UPON THEM ALL

UPON THEM ALL

ORDINARY PEOPLE, EXTRAORDINARY PURPOSE:
TRUE STORIES TO IGNITE YOUR FAITH.

ELLIANA OLIVIA

Upon Them All

First paperback edition March 2025

Published by Bay Horse Publishing House

Minneapolis, Minnesota

ISBN-13 (eBook): 979-8-9896724-9-3

ISBN-13 (Print): 979-8-9896724-5-5

Library of Congress Control Number: 2025906533

This book is a work of nonfiction. While the events and experiences shared are true to the best of the storytellers' recollection, certain names and identifying details have been changed to protect the privacy of individuals involved.

Visit the author's website at https://www.ellianaolivia.com/

To my grandmother, whose joy and faith taught me that a life lived with God is the most joyous adventure of all.

To all my relatives, whose journeys have fanned my faith into flame and taught me that, with God all things are possible.

May these testimonies encourage your faith as they did mine.

CONTENTS

THE WHO, THE WHAT, AND THE WHY

This book is a collection of testimonies from a number of my relatives. It is an account of the miraculous events that took place from the 1920s through the early 2000s. My initial motivation in collecting these stories was to preserve them for future generations of our family. However, as I began investigating and interviewing family members, this project blossomed into something unexpected. In the process of writing about these testimonies, I found myself reflecting on the values that each one had taught me, so I decided to share it all in the form of a book. Many of these stories that I present to you in this compilation are what shaped the very foundation of my faith as a young child.

I think it's interesting that the Bible is written mainly in the form of stories—real stories—of people who encountered the power of the living God. These very accounts within the Bible that have been passed down from generation to generation have been and still are influencing the faith of believers today. Since the beginning, mankind has been recording their stories of the extraordinary experiences that they have had with God. If this is how God interacted with people in the Bible, then what's to say His ways have changed? He is still the same God as described in the pages of the Scriptures, and He is still visiting people in miraculous ways to this very day. My hope is that we continue to share the testimonies of God's goodness in our lives, so that future generations will come to know Jesus as the *One and Only* miracle-working God.

While this book is a collection of multiple stories told by different family members, I have written each one from the first-person perspective so that it feels as if you are sitting down over coffee and cookies with my extended relatives to hear about these remarkable moments for yourself. I have done my best to present these stories with accuracy while honoring my relatives and those included in the following pages. I have changed a few of the names for privacy, but none of the details or facts have been altered. This is the real story of how our family came to know about the transformative power of Jesus. There were many unusual miracles that took place, but I have personally witnessed that the fruit of these events were not "fanatical beliefs" but rather a deep-founded faith that was rooted in Christ alone.

Since I am writing about my family, I can also attest to the fact that none of them were perfect, but I think knowing that they also had shortcomings, just like you and me, brings all the more glory to God in each story. Recording all these miraculous salvations reminds me of the words of Paul when he writes in 1 Corinthians 2:4–5 (NIV) that he did not win people to Christ because of fancy and persuasive words, "but with a demonstration of the Spirit's power, so that your faith might not rest on human wisdom, but on God's power." What I am really trying to convey through these accounts is how God loves to partner with ordinary, everyday believers to expand His Kingdom. While some names are mentioned, they aren't always emphasized—this is intentional. The heart of these testimonies isn't to spotlight any particular anointed man or woman, but to reveal the Spirit of God at work through those simply willing to follow His lead.

At the end of each chapter, I share my own reflections in the "Author's Notes" section. These are separate from what each person shared, but I included these insights to ignite your heart for the harvest! I didn't necessarily intend this book to become centered on the theme of evangelism, but the more I wrote, the more I was provoked to see a generation end the labor shortage.

I had originally picked out a different name for this book, but while I was in graduate school learning about the Old Testament prophets, I found it very interesting to hear more about the context behind the Book of Joel. During that time period, the elite men of society would recite a prayer of thanksgiving to God daily. These men would thank God that they were not born a *gentile*, a *woman*, or a *slave*. So, you can imagine the leaders were not exactly pleased when Joel prophesied that God was planning to shake up their societal hierarchy.

> "Then, after doing all those things, I will pour out my Spirit upon all people. Your sons and daughters will prophesy. Your old men will dream dreams, and your young men will see visions. In those days I will pour out my Spirit even on servants—men and women alike."

JOEL 2:28–29 NLT

The Messiah came so that His Spirit could be poured out upon *all* people and now in Christ:

> "There is neither Jew nor Gentile, neither slave nor free, nor is there male and female, for you are all one in Christ Jesus. If you belong to Christ, then you are Abraham's seed, and heirs according to the promise."

GALATIANS 3:28–29 NIV

We become heirs to the promise if we call on the name of Jesus to save and redeem us. No matter what country you come from, how old you are, or what you do for a living, Christ came to pour out His Spirit upon *you* too. This profound reality is the very heart of this book. I hope that, as you read the following chapters, you will catch a glimpse into the heart of God to see that He truly desires to pour out His Spirit *upon them all.*

CHAPTER 1
HELL, CATS, AND CRIME
ARE NO MATCH FOR GOD

How did I come to the Lord? Well, that's quite a story. It really all started with my dad. He would come home drunk most nights and beat me almost half to death. One time, when I was around fifteen, he assaulted me so severely that I lost consciousness. My back broke under the pressure of his raging fists. They brought me to the hospital to try to help, but the beating left my spine badly damaged. From then on, I decided I couldn't take it anymore, and I ran away from home with my boyfriend in the 1950s.

Because of all of this, I ended up getting married when I was really young, and it wasn't long before I was delivering our very first child in the hospital. My back still gave me a lot of trouble, and now, attempting to deliver an eleven-pound baby felt impossible with the kind of pain I was in. Most women were still delivering babies naturally in those days because a C-section was still considered a relatively new kind of surgery. It was risky and only used in emergencies at that point. Once the doctors realized that the baby was stuck, they tried to perform an emergency C-section, but it was too late.

Between my back injury and all the hours in labor, my body gave way. Blackness covered my eyes as I lost consciousness, and then an even darker shadow flooded my soul as I began to descend. I saw that I was sinking into a tunnel that spiraled down and down and down. Slowly, I slid deeper into the darkness. The most wretched smell rose from the bottom. I could barely stand the stench. Shadows started to appear out of the side of the enclosure, clasping and grabbing at me. They couldn't wait to have their way with me. The demons grew more fierce and the smell even more potent. I tried to climb up, but I couldn't. I was drowning in dread and fear. There was no way out. I was on my way to hell with no hope of escape.

Until I cried upon that precious, holy, saving name of Jesus—with all my might, I cried out to God. I prayed, asking if He would give me a second chance. Suddenly, my descent into the vile pit came to a complete stop, and with one great lift, God pulled my soul right out of the entrance of hell.

I opened my eyes and saw a thin white sheet lying over my face. Then, I heard my husband crying somewhere nearby. I ripped the sheet off of me and sat up.

"What are you crying about? I'm the one who just died and went to hell!"

———

Everything about my life changed since that day the Lord rescued me from eternal death. I knew Jesus wasn't just a "religion" because I had experienced firsthand the power of His redemption. I knew that sickness, demons, and even hell itself were no match for God. My heart burned for others to experience the saving power of Jesus.

In the 1980s, I took a job as a high school teacher in Pleasanton, Texas, and I saw it as the perfect opportunity to share the gospel with the next generation. Even though I wasn't "technically" supposed to be talking about my faith at work, that never stopped me. I wanted my students to know the truth.

After school one day, several girls from my class approached me to ask if they could hear more about this Jesus that I was always talking about. I knew most of them had come from broken homes and needed someone to talk to about what was weighing on their hearts. So, that day, we had our very first Bible study meeting.

There were many kids at our school who longed to feel like they belonged somewhere. They were like lost sheep, looking for a shepherd to lovingly care for them. You could see in their eyes that they were hungry for God. Their hearts were searching for the love that only He offers. As the news spread of our little meeting, more kids wanted to join. After class, kids would pile into the back of my truck, and I'd drive them all to my house to talk about Jesus. The Bible study grew and grew until my little trailer house was packed with kids.

———

One of the students in the special ed class at school had heard about what was happening at our Bible studies and wanted to come join. He had a hard time learning since he could barely read or write, but what he lacked in brain-power, he made up for in ferocity. The entire school feared him. He was small in stature, around five foot five at best, but when he walked down the hallway, the kids parted like the Red Sea. No one wanted to be caught near Gabriel. He was one of the toughest and most dangerous kids, not only in high school but also in the entire county. Everything surrounding him was bad news until he decided to come to our meeting.

As I was sharing about Jesus, Gabriel started to manifest. The demons didn't exactly like my message, so they decided they were going to try to kill me. Little Gabriel, raging with demonic strength, picked up one of the couches in my house. He held the entire couch above his head with a murderous look in his eyes. He was full of all sorts of demons, but I knew if God could deliver me straight out of the pit of hell, then He could do the same thing for Gabriel.

As he was about to throw the couch at me, I looked him straight in the eyes and said in a loud, authoritative voice, "Put that couch down, in the name of Jesus!"

For a moment, Gabriel stood there, looking puzzled. Then, he gently set the couch down and calmly walked toward me to sit down. In a very calm tone, I assured him that the next thing I was about to say was not directed at him.

Again loudly, I said, "Demon, in the name of Jesus, get out of him now!"

He was instantly delivered, and his following conversion to Christ was radical. After that day, he became like my right-hand man. He helped lead many of the other "tough" kids at school to the Lord. He also started to learn to read by reading Scripture. He would bring his Bible to school, walking down those same halls with his beloved book tucked under his arm. Shortly after he was born again, his grades started improving, and they were able to transfer him out of the special ed classes into the standard grade with the rest of his peers. The more he learned about the Bible, the more brilliant he became. In a short time, he ended up becoming one of the smartest kids in high school. Even the teachers noticed how drastically Gabriel had changed.

When they asked me what happened to him, I would tell them, "It's Jesus."

———

As more healings and deliverances took place, the youth group grew even more. Gabriel and others were bringing more and more of their friends. I had no idea how I could possibly fit any more kids in my house.

The school principal had a friend, Mr. Wheeler, who happened to own a warehouse. When the principal heard about my "problem" with the Bible study, he thought maybe he could convince his friend to let us use the space since he knew it wasn't being used for anything else. Mr. Wheeler was hesitant at first, but in the end, he agreed to let us use the warehouse. Our youth group grew to over a hundred students after we moved into the building. A lot of them came from troubled homes. It was a safe space for them to ask the hard questions of life and faith. Many of them encountered Jesus in powerful ways.

Entire families were coming to the Lord because of what was happening to the kids at school. The crime rates were drastically dropping because numerous students were getting saved and delivered. The community started to change so much that news about what was happening spread to other cities. City officials from a neighboring town had come to investigate the sudden decline in crime. The sheriff called me in to explain to the interviewers about the revival that was breaking out in the high school. Our meeting ended up making the headlines in San Antonio because the crime rates had plummeted. Our stats served as a testament to the transformative power of Jesus.

After many fruitful years in Pleasanton, transforming the roughest and toughest kids into warriors of the Kingdom of Heaven, I relocated closer to the border in Roma, Texas. I also took a job teaching in the high school there. It wasn't long before I became acquainted with our new church. I teamed up with the local youth pastor, and together, we started to see the youth group in Roma flourish.

On one occasion, the church called me and asked if I could come and pray for one of the high school girls who wouldn't stop demonically manifesting at the service. When I arrived, I saw several people hovering over the girl off to the side of the altar. They had tried to cast the demons out for over an hour to no avail. She was lying there, eyes rolled back, foaming at the mouth, looking like she was on the brink of death. She shifted between a state of unconsciousness and speaking in hideous demonic voices.

Her newly saved friend, who had brought this young girl to church, was also standing off to the side, crying hysterically because she thought her friend was dying. Being a brand-new Christian, she had never seen anyone demonically manifest or get delivered before. She had no idea that her friend had been into witchcraft, which explained how those evil forces had a grip over the girl.

The pastors told her they were calling someone in who could get this demon out. She expected someone big, strong, and intimidating, but to her surprise, here comes her local high school teacher. She had no idea how someone so small in stature and unsuspecting in appearance could kick out a demon this fierce, but there was no demon that could ever intimidate me because I had the bold assurance of *Who* lived inside of me. I knelt down beside the girl and gently placed my hand on her face.

I rebuked the demon and said, "You are not going to speak to me. I don't want to speak to you. I want to speak to her."

The girl regained consciousness, and I walked her through a prayer for deliverance from the witchcraft. She renounced the demon and kicked it out herself. She was perfectly set free.

————

Working together with the church, the youth group continued to grow. We saw numerous kids saved, healed, and delivered. It wasn't long before I was praying for the high school staff as well. I found out that our superintendent had severe back pain. I prayed for him, and he was instantly healed. The miracle impacted him so much that he gave me free rein to talk about God as much as I wanted at school.

So much happened during those years; God swept through our high school. I loved praying for the kids, especially the troubled ones. I would talk real straight with them about God. Sometimes, it was tough love, but it always melted their hearts. The kids were hungry to hear the real deal; they longed to know Jesus as the Redeemer, the Healer, and the Savior. They were filled with hope as they witnessed with their own eyes how truly anything is possible with God. I wanted to show these kids that when you walk with God, you can touch heaven and make hell tremble.

The revival spread so much throughout the school that the football players wanted me to come and pray for them before every game. If you know anything about Texas, then you know that football is a big deal around here. All the players would start lining up after the first period on their game days. One by one, I would pray for them; even the toughest kids would come to receive prayer.

They always asked me to come to their games because they could sense the presence of Jesus. Before each game, I would tell them, "Whether you win or lose, you represent God out there, and God is going to keep you safe."

———

While some students were happy to hear about Jesus, others resented me for it. I remember one semester when I had a particularly challenging group of kids in my computer class. One day after school, I noticed a few of them waiting around. They approached me to ask if we could talk. I was always happy to help my students, but I noticed that their demeanor conveyed some sort of trepidation.

I was taken aback by their first question: "Mrs. Garcia, who lives with you?"

I wondered why they would be asking such a thing. At the time, only my son and I lived in our home but no one else. When I inquired why they wanted to know, they let out a sheepish confession of how they had gone to my house yesterday because they wanted to "egg it." Apparently, they were fed up with me and came up with a "brilliant" plan to vandalize my property to get back at me. When they had brought the eggs over to my house, they saw tall, well-built men standing outside. Immediately, they turned and ran, fearing for their safety. They never threw a single egg. The moment the kids had confessed the story, I knew that it was angels who were protecting my house that day.

————

We continued to see miracles happen in our youth group, but one of the most unique ones involved a small white cat who was owned by a little boy named Rafael. He had named the cat "Diablito," Spanish for "little devil," because, indeed, that cat acted like a little devil. It had reddish-pink eyes and would scratch at anyone who came near it. The only person who could hold him was Rafael, but as soon as he left for school, the cat would go berserk. Several times, his mom begged him to get rid of the cat because she was scared of it, but he kept insisting on keeping it since someone had given it to him as a gift.

One day, when he came home from school, he found his cat lying on the brink of death. It crushed him to see his beloved pet so sick. He came over to our house, devastated by the whole situation.

With tears streaming down his face, he said, "Mrs. Garcia, something is wrong with my cat."

I insisted, "Well, why don't you bring the cat over, and we'll pray for it."

He left the house and returned with the cat in his arms.

He set it down, but it barely moved. I ran my hand

across the little animal lying there lifeless. "What do you call the cat?"

"Diablito."

I knew exactly what that meant, so I said, "Oh, no. That won't do. We're going to have to change that name."

I prayed for the cat, and he scooped its small body up in his arms and walked home. I didn't see Rafael for a few days after that.

Then I heard someone from afar yell in a panic, "Mrs. Garcia! Mrs. Garcia! I have to tell you something!"

Here was Rafael, running as fast as he could toward me. I assumed his cat had died because of his frantic demeanor.

"Mrs. Garcia, you have to come see my cat! It's a miracle! It's a miracle! He's gotten all better now, and he's doing great! His sickness went away, and now he's not even scratching people anymore. He's all nice and loving, but the weirdest thing happened! You have to come and see!"

So I went with him to see the cat. When I walked in, the little white cat perked up and stared at me. He seemed to be doing much better, but this time, instead of looking into those devilish red eyes, bright blue ones gazed back at me.

"Mrs. Garcia, I decided to rename him Milagro." (*Milagro* is Spanish for "miracle.")

His whole family came to know the Lord because they witnessed how God had transformed that cat. Many of the kids at school also got saved because of the change they saw. Who knew that one cat's deliverance could lead to so many salvations?

AUTHOR'S NOTES:

Elva's faith was audacious. She knew if God said it, then He was going to do it. Her bold confidence in God changed entire communities. Her conversion to Christ was radical, but what I really love about this story is hearing about the impact she made as a local high school teacher. My heart in writing this book was to capture the stories of "ordinary" people living extraordinary lives because they believed in a miracle-working God. Elva nor *anyone* else in the following pages was a "preacher," or "evangelist," or "missionary" in the way the church often defines those terms today. Yet, they all preached the gospel, evangelized their communities, and adopted their workplaces as their mission field because they knew God had given them a light that could not be hidden—a treasure that could not be buried.

To be a Christian means to be "Christlike." In the West, however, it seems as if we have reduced being "like Christ" to moral character and church attendance. Although these things are important, the early church had a much different understanding of what it meant to be a disciple of Jesus. In Jewish culture, the term *disciple* was not merely about listening to someone's teaching; rather, the focus was to become as they are. They were to adopt the lifestyles of their masters by *doing as they do*. According to Acts 10:38 (NIV), Jesus "…went around doing good and healing all who were under the power of the devil…" and all of His disciples followed suit. Jesus not only transformed their character but He also baptized them with the power of the Holy Spirit to continue to carry out the assignment of freeing those who were under the oppression of the kingdom of darkness.

During the period of the early church, the world identified Christians by the *Presence* that they carried with them. How do you think the people knew to bring the ill near Peter so that his shadow could heal them? (See Acts 5:15–16.) Or to take some of Paul's fabric over to the sick and demonized to be set free? (See Acts 19:11–12.) It was because they noticed when you got around "those Christians," diseases and demons left. The church walked in God's power because they understood that whoever believed in Jesus would do the works He had done and would do even greater things than these because Jesus went to be with the Father. In His final hours, Jesus commissioned His church to continue His work by asking in His name so that His (and our) Father may be continually glorified through these works. (See John 14:12–14.)

As Christians today, we still serve the same God. The assignment hasn't changed, and neither has God's power. We are the very body of Christ at work on the earth to help those in our generation who are under the oppression of the devil. The evil in this world is not something that can be overcome in our strength and goodwill. The crime rate dropped in Pleasanton not because everyone started attending church; it was because all the demons started getting kicked out of town! Our battle is "...not against flesh and blood, but against the rulers, against the authorities, against the powers of this dark world and against the spiritual forces of evil in the heavenly realms" (Ephesians 6:12 NIV). The world needs what we carry; they need the power of God to redeem them. No matter what problems your community may be facing, remember: *hell, cats, and crime are no match for God!*

CHAPTER 2
I DON'T KNOW WHAT IN THE WORLD SHE'S GOT, BUT I WANT IT!

In the spring of 1971, my husband, our kids, and I went on a vacation to escape the frigid Minnesota winter. During our trip, my husband began to experience recurring chest pains. He told me that when we returned home, he would like to find a church that anoints with oil and prays for healing the way the Bible teaches. Hearing this immediately made me anxious. Our pastor and even our parents would tell us to have nothing to do with those "tongues-speaking Pentecostals." Constantly, they drilled into us that the gifts of the Spirit were *not* for Christians today. In their mind, the only true way to follow God was by obeying "the little black book." This was a list of rules we needed to follow in order to avoid going to hell. We had no idea that we could have an actual relationship with Jesus. I didn't even know God knew my name. I was just hoping—praying that I might be good enough to make it. That's all I wanted. This fear constantly tormented me in my nightmares.

When my husband finally found a church where he heard miracles were happening, he decided to go to one of the services. Because of my upbringing, I thought he was going to be led astray by some fanatical church. I was still troubled by the thought of him going. My best defense was to join him in attending the service so I could stop him from getting mixed up in all this wild teaching that our pastor always told us was dangerous.

When we arrived at the church, I was surprised by the warmth of the atmosphere. I could feel the presence of God so strongly that I was moved to tears. After the service, my husband went up to the front to receive prayer, and I went with him. I was deeply touched by every word the pastor had prayed for him. When he finished, the thought came into my mind that I should probably receive prayer too. Everything about this church began to melt away my preconceived notions that I had come in with. It didn't seem like such a bad idea after all to receive prayer. I thought, *Well it can't hurt me, but it probably won't help me either.*

I had suffered from migraines since I was a young child, and to make things worse, I was in a car accident that left me in horrible pain. I was on medication for the last few years to try to subside some of the symptoms, but most of the time, even the pills barely helped. When I received prayer, not only did I get completely healed but I also got delivered from the spirit of fear, unbelief, doubt, tension, anxiety, nerves, and migraines! I could physically feel the spirit of fear and migraines leave my body. They leaped from my stomach all the way to the top of my head and then left. The rest I knew were gone! After taking care of the devil's handiwork, the pastor prayed for me to be filled with the love, joy, and peace of Jesus. I was so filled with the Holy Spirit that I laughed and cried the entire way home.

I tried to go to sleep that evening, but I couldn't. I stayed up the entire night playing the organ and worshipping Jesus. For the first time ever, I knew without a shadow of a doubt that I was indeed one of God's beloved children. The peace that flooded my soul was unlike anything else I had ever experienced in my entire life. God saved me, healed me, and delivered me! After I was filled with the Holy Spirit, I had an entire week of dreams, visions, and encounters with Jesus. I call it "my week with the Lord." (If you would like to read about these in detail, they are written in *In His Hand* by Phyllis Olson.)

During this week, I was barely eating, drinking, or sleeping. I would often be slain in the Spirit for hours, and then the next thing you know, I would be laughing because I was so overcome with the joy of Jesus. Then I would receive a different vision and be moved to tears over what I had just seen. It was one thing after another. God also led me through many moments of inner healing during that week. He addressed the deep wounds that had weighed on my heart for years. There were so many things that happened in such a short period of time.

Different friends and family would stop by to check on me. Some were very worried, while others recognized that this was the Lord baptizing me with the Holy Spirit. One of my sister's friends, who had already been baptized in the Spirit as well, came over to visit with me. My sister, her friend, and I were all sitting around in a room while I was catching them up on everything God had been showing me. Then, suddenly, I started to see in the spiritual realm. I was in awe when I caught a glimpse of what my sister's friend looked like. Her spirit was absolutely beautiful, overflowing with the presence of God.

Over and over, I kept saying, "Kathy, you're just beautiful! Just beautiful!"

Suddenly, the joy of the Lord flooded the room, and we broke into holy laughter. We couldn't contain ourselves; we were rolling all over the place. My mom had also stopped by that day, and she walked over to the room to see what was happening. When she peered in the door to see what all the commotion was about, she went back into the hall and started crying. Although she was born again, she was taught the same things I was growing up. She didn't yet understand that this joy was from the Lord. She thought I had gotten mixed up in something bad. I honestly felt sorry for her. I really wanted to try to explain what was going on, but at the time, I barely understood what was happening myself. When I finally calmed down enough, I tried to go and comfort her, but she was so upset.

She said to me, "Sometimes you lie there and you can't even walk! Then the next minute, you're laughing and dancing! I don't understand what's wrong with you!"

Even though I was barely physically functioning, my spirit was alive and well for the first time in my life. God was completely transforming my heart, my perspective, and my entire life. He was showing me things beyond what I ever could have imagined.

The day after my mom came by, I received one of the most impactful open visions. I was lying down, looking up at the ceiling, and instantly, my surroundings changed. There was the most beautiful paradise before me—it was heaven. Every detail was absolute perfection, from the blades of grass to the gorgeous trees. Then I started to see colors that I had never seen before. The sheer magnificence of the vision transcended anything I could comprehend. I was so captivated by the beauty that it brought me to the point of feeling as though I might die if I continued on any further. I asked the Lord to stop the vision, but I instantly regretted this as the image before me was swept away. Even this brief glimpse into heaven etched an everlasting longing in me for the beautiful promised land that awaits every believer.

Shortly after I had seen the vision, one of my friends from the church I grew up in stopped by the house. She wanted to come see me because her mother had told her that everyone has got to start praying for me because I am in "big trouble." Apparently, a rumor had started in the church that I was having a nervous breakdown. The people had heard that I was prophesying and receiving visions. So they assumed I was out of my mind, but in reality, I was just out of theirs. My dear old friend wanted to see for herself. When she came over, I excitedly told her all about the vision I had recently seen and everything I had been experiencing that week. I was so happy I could barely stand it! She sat there and watched me for about an hour.

When she left, she told everyone, "I don't know what in the world she's got, but I want it!"

It wasn't long before she was baptized in the Spirit too. The Holy Spirit began to pour His Spirit out *upon us all*. It was unlike any other time we had experienced. My siblings, as well as my friends, started to catch fire for Jesus. We were seeing more happen in a matter of weeks than we had for years.

At the very end of my week with the Lord, God gave me His heart for the great harvest.

He told me, "Just be available, and be filled with My love."

Simple, isn't it? God is looking for *willing* workers who are filled with His love. When we choose to make ourselves available, His Spirit will lead us to reach those around us. It's incredible what can happen! I have personally experienced the power of this when I asked the Lord to open up opportunities to share with people. One evening, I opened up my Bible to a random page and began reading this verse in John 14:

> "And I will do whatever you ask in my name, so that the Father may be glorified in the Son. You may ask me for anything in my name, and I will do it."
>
> JOHN 14:13–14 NIV

As I was reading it, the words flowed out of me, "Lord, if Your Word is true, then I ask to share about what You've done in my life with a thousand people this year and pray with one hundred people to receive Jesus."

It was a bold prayer, but now that I had been transformed I had a longing for more. My hunger extended beyond just "reading" about the Word; I wanted to actually experience it. It's alive and active, and it has the ability to change our lives when we partner with it.

———

In the months that followed, I was invited to all sorts of Bible studies and events as news of my story spread.

I remember my aunt Laura called me one day and said, "We have one of the best Bible studies. Why don't you come by someday? It's really good."

I assured her that I would stop in when I could, but life

was very full with the kids and everything going on. I wasn't able to make it over there yet, so she called me again. This time, she wasn't asking; she was insisting. I finally set aside time in my crazy schedule and headed over to the Bible study.

When I walked in and started socializing with the ladies, one of them remarked, "We can't wait to hear your story!"

I was shocked. I wondered how they even knew that. I thought my aunt must have been saying something to the women at the meeting. That's when it hit me that I hadn't just been invited to come and join but to actually speak. Even though it was unexpected, I had a great deal of fun talking about my week with the Lord and praying for different people. It stirred their faith to hear about the experience I had with God. As I told them about what God delivered me from, people would get powerfully touched by Jesus.

———

There were many times when people would ask me to come and share my testimony in their homes. I remember one time I had just finished speaking at a teen's group, and afterward, the leader asked if I would be willing to come to her house to share with her nine adult children. She had also been recently filled with the Holy Spirit, and she longed for her family to encounter Jesus the way she and I had experienced.

When she had received prayer to be baptized in the Spirit, she was so filled up with joy that she began to laugh. Before all of this, she was a very scrupulous woman who thought it was irreverent to laugh in church, but now she just couldn't stop. She laughed and laughed until she was embarrassed. No matter how hard she tried, she couldn't suppress the laughter that was bubbling up from inside of her. The Holy Spirit was freeing her in that moment and filling her up with His joy!

She tried to share about this with her husband, but he had more of the quiet kind of faith, which he thought was meant to be silent and internal. She tried to talk about it with her kids when they would stop by the house, but none of them were really interested in what she was saying. Although they were also believers, they didn't quite have the revelation yet that being a follower wasn't about an adherence to a certain doctrine but rather a *personal* relationship with Jesus. After she had heard about how God delivered me from the mindset of thinking being a Christian was about following a set of rules, she thought it might ignite some fire in the hearts of her kids to pursue a relationship with Jesus.

One of the kids, named Sue, was planning on leaving while I was there after she had heard that her mom had invited someone over to talk about the Lord. (Funnily enough, she ended up becoming one of my dear friends and ministry partners.) Sue had been cleaning the house all day and preparing everything for the meeting. She thought that the moment I saw her in her work clothes, I would take one look at her and say, "You sinner!" She expected me to be a big ol' mean woman with a righteous vengeance. Despite her plan to slip out unnoticed, I arrived just before she had left the house. When she caught a glimpse of me, she noticed that I was merely a short little woman who laughed a lot and seemed quite normal. Intrigued by my demeanor, she decided she would stay...just for a little while to hear what I had to say.

Altogether, there were about fifteen people there. Most of the kids were present, as well as the parents and a few neighbors. They all sat around and listened intently to every detail.

When I had finished, one of them asked, "Well...can I have the Holy Spirit?"

"Oh, yes!" I remarked.

One after another stood up to be filled with the Spirit, including Sue. When I had prayed for her, she later said, that it was as if scales fell off her eyes and everything became brighter. For the first time in her life, she could feel the nearness of Jesus. Everything about her life changed, and she went on to lead many people to the Lord. She would often be praying for coworkers at the office, and she also went around ministering to different groups with me. We had years of fun together seeing people encounter the power of God!

After most of the kids had been prayed for at the meeting, the father got up and walked over to me.

He said, "Well, I really do need this too!"

All the kids in the room begin to clap, shout, and cheer. They were so excited for their dad to get baptized in the Holy Spirit. It was such a heartwarming and humorous moment to witness. After that meeting, they were completely transformed. God loves to pour out His Spirit upon entire families!

———

As more and more of our community were getting baptized in the Spirit, everything about our lives was changing, even the most ordinary events like baby showers. My sister was pregnant at the time, and her shower ended up turning into a wonderful prayer meeting. The power of God was in the house, and people started getting healed and delivered. Everyone started to invite others to come because so much was happening.

One of my friends, Donna, had called her husband and said, "You have to come down here and experience this!"

He wasn't filled with the Spirit yet, and the idea of coming to a baby shower that had turned into a prayer meeting didn't necessarily pique his interest, so he told his wife no. Shortly after she called, he came bursting through the door at the shower. His wife wondered what suddenly changed his mind.

"What happened?" she inquired.

"Well, right after you called, the bedroom door opened all on its own. Then the lights started coming on in the house. It freaked me out so much that I came straight here."

The Lord has peculiar ways of drawing us to Him. He can use anything and do anything to accomplish His purposes. It wasn't long before Donna's husband caught the fire of the Holy Spirit too!

As we were praying for different people, my brother stopped in with his son. He had been having a lot of problems getting along with the other kids at school. The school administrator insisted that they get a counselor for him because he was always getting into trouble. When we prayed for deliverance, a big smile swept across his face. He lifted his hands in the air as Jesus flooded his heart with peace. He was so happy after that. God set him free from whatever spirit was tormenting him, and he never had another problem at school after that day.

It was such a fun time seeing God move at that baby shower. It went on for hours as we ministered to different people. There ain't no party like a Holy Ghost party!

———

Although I had forgotten about my little bold prayer, God hadn't. He was keeping track the whole time.

About a month after I had prayed that, He told me, "Get up and write down all the names of the people you have shared your testimony with this month."

I grabbed a pen and paper, and I wrote down 115 names nonstop. It humbled me to see all those names listed in just *one* month. God was fulfilling His Word and answering my prayer. I could hardly believe it. I knew before long that He would exceed beyond what I had asked.

Everywhere I went, the Lord opened up opportunities to share with people. While I was shopping for groceries, I ran into one of my old friends from high school. Back in the day, I knew she wasn't a Christian, but she was always such a happy person to be around. As we started catching up, she asked what had been going on in my life recently.

I started to tell her about my testimony, and she interjected, "Oh my goodness, you got saved! So did I!"

It was a great deal of fun to share our stories with one another of how we had found the Lord later in life.

She continued on, "I go to this wonderful Bible study. Would you be willing to come and share your story with our group?"

Of course I agreed, and the next week I went to the meeting. After I finished talking, I started praying for the different ladies who came forward. There was one very classy woman who approached me to give me a hug.

As she did, she whispered in my ear, "Nobody here knows it, but I've been an alcoholic for twenty-five years."

I prayed softly in her ear so that no one else could hear. I asked Jesus to set her free and transform her life.

A few days later, as I was going through the messages on my answering machine, I heard over the speaker, "I'M FREE! I'M FREE! I'M FREE!"

It was the woman who had been an alcoholic for all those years, and God had set her free in an instant. We ended up going to lunch, and she shared with me how the Lord told her that if she went up to receive prayer, then He would set her free. When we choose to follow the prompting of the Holy Spirit, He can do more in five seconds than we can do in twenty-five years.

————

After about six months went by, the Lord prompted me to write down all the names of everyone I had led to Jesus this time. Nonstop, I wrote down sixty-five names of those I had personally prayed with for salvation. I was so humbled as I stared back at this list as well.

I said, "Oh, Lord, I will never ask You to prove Your Word again. Now I know it is true."

In a year, the Lord surpassed what I had asked for! I shared my testimony with over a thousand people, and I prayed with more than one hundred to receive Jesus. God did it! He answered my prayer. He was showing me that His Word is indeed true, and He will open up the opportunities to work in the harvest field if we ask for them. This whole experience forever changed me, and the Lord transformed everything about my life. To this day, it is my great privilege to tell people about God's miracle-working power!

AUTHOR'S NOTES:

When I have heard people speak about the Great Commission, they often nail this part perfectly: "Therefore go and make disciples of all nations, baptizing them in the name of the Father and of the Son and of the Holy Spirit..." However, it is crucial to remember that this sentence doesn't end here. That keyword *and* connects the following sentence to the Great Commission as well: "...and teaching them to obey everything I have commanded you. And surely I am with you always, to the very end of the age" (Matthew 28:19–20 NIV).

I remember while I was reading this verse, I wondered what exactly the "everything" was that Jesus had commanded the *disciples*. I carefully examined each of the Gospel accounts, combing through every passage where Jesus spoke to His followers in an 'imperative mood.' In the original language, speaking in an 'imperative mood' would be the equivalent of giving someone a *command*. There are two commands that Jesus gave that I want to highlight in this section.

The first one I would like to discuss is one that is given several times throughout the Gospel accounts, but I think Matthew 10:7–8 (NIV) encapsulates it best: "As you go, proclaim this message: 'The kingdom of heaven has come near.' Heal the sick, raise the dead, cleanse those who have leprosy, drive out demons. Freely you have received; freely give." It could be easy to dismiss this as simply instructions given to the twelve. However, it is crucial to note that Jesus reiterates this when He commissions the seventy-two to go out into the harvest field as well. The deliberate repetition brings to light a blueprint of how Jesus wanted His followers to expand His Kingdom. Furthermore, the entire Book of Acts illustrates this blueprint as the early church demonstrated how God's Kingdom was to be multiplied for future generations to come. This command, which was further solidified in the Gospel of Mark, was intended to be passed on to every believer so that *all the world in every generation* could hear the good news:

> "He said to them, 'Go into all the world and preach the gospel to all creation. Whoever believes and is baptized will be saved, but whoever does not believe will be condemned. And these signs will accompany those who believe: In my name they will drive out demons; they will speak in new tongues; they will pick up snakes with their hands; and when they drink deadly poison, it will not hurt them at all; they will place their hands on sick people, and they will get well.'"

MARK 16:15–18 NIV

It doesn't say these signs will accompany *only* "the apostles." It says these signs will accompany "those who BELIEVE." Are you a believer? Then this verse is as relevant and true today as it was for those who wrote those very words. As you've read in this story, "these signs" followed ordinary everyday believers. If they didn't, then there are many salvations in this story that would not have happened. If they didn't, then Phyllis might still be oppressed by her fear and pain. If they didn't, then that woman may still be bound by a spirit of addiction, secretly drinking her life away. God wants His people to be free from sickness, addiction, demons, fear, and everything that the fall set into motion. His gospel is not merely a "one-day" hope; it is an "on earth as it is in heaven" because the Kingdom of Heaven is here! It is something we can experience right now. He doesn't want us to stay bound until we die and go to heaven one day. He came to save us and set us free right here and now!

"So if the Son sets you free, you will be free indeed."

JOHN 8:36 NIV

The second command I want to highlight was given right before He commissioned the seventy-two to go out and preach in Luke 10. Jesus told them, "…Ask the Lord of the harvest, therefore, to send out workers into his harvest field" (Luke 10:2 NIV). This is also a vital command that they would have passed on to the next generation of disciples. Yet, when you think about praying this, do you include yourself? Will you be part of the answer to God's heart cry to reach His lost people? God longs to pour out His love, His healing, and His redemption through *you*!

Pray for even more laborers for the harvest, but also pray that you might be one of them as Phyllis did in this story. Whether she realized it at the time or not, her prayer was partnering with God's desire to bring in the bountiful harvest! When you choose to partner with God and ask Him to move mightily through you, you may be surprised by how He does! God loves to go above and beyond what we could even think, ask, or imagine. It is so much fun to be a laborer in God's Kingdom, and the benefits are great! (See Psalm 103:2–5.) God longs for us all to be part of the harvest time!

CHAPTER 3
SERIOUSNESS IS NOT A FRUIT OF THE SPIRIT, BUT JOY IS!

Something had ignited within me. A great longing for Jesus began to stir in me after I witnessed how the Holy Spirit was being poured out upon our family. I wanted to be baptized in the Spirit. I went to a church to visit with a pastor who I thought could pray for me to be filled. Instead, he suggested that I come back another time when the elders were there. I remember leaving his office feeling disappointed that day. That momentary setback filled my eyes with tears. I was so hungry to be filled with the Holy Spirit; all I wanted was more of God. When I got home, I didn't even want to go inside and talk with my wife; I just sat in the car and wept.

A few days later, I received a call from a dear friend. She told me she was going to a prayer meeting that night at someone's house. She invited me to come and even offered to pick me up. I agreed, and off we went. I was astonished to see a monstrously large house on Lake of the Isles as we drove up the driveway. It was stunning. We walked inside and made our way into the large living room, where about fifty people were gathered.

The speaker that night was a gentleman who had worked on the mission field with a courageous missionary known for sneaking Bibles into Russia. He would alter his car and fill it to the brim with the Holy Word of God. Whenever the guards tried to look inside, they could never find any of those Bibles. His courage and bravery on the mission field inspired me as I listened to story after story of how God was moving powerfully in oppressed countries.

After the meeting, a woman approached me and asked, "Are you filled with the Spirit?"

"No," I said.

"Do you want to be?"

Excitement filled my whole being. "Yes!"

She cued for the missionary who had been sharing that night to come over and lay hands on me. Instantly, I was filled with the Holy Spirit. I just knew I had been filled! I didn't feel anything physically happen in my body when the missionary prayed for me, but afterward, I felt absolutely exuberant! That night, I had received three words in tongues. I had no idea what I was saying, but I kept repeating them over and over.

When I went home, I could barely contain my excitement. I was so caught up in the Lord that I don't even know what I said or what I did. Later, my wife told me that I was lying in bed with my hands up the whole night, speaking in this funny language. I couldn't recall doing any of that. It was the Lord who had been filling me up even while I was sleeping. God was continually pouring out His joy upon me because in His presence, there is the fullness of joy (see Psalm 16:11).

It reminded me of the times we would go to the altar when we were kids. We had no idea what we were doing.

Going to the altar in our extremely legalistic church was solely for "repentance." While I was up at the altar, I would have a sense of joy because I felt near to God for just a moment, but sadly, I never knew I could live that way all the time. No one ever told us about how to become born again. I thought I was simply a sinner separated from God, hoping I didn't mess up too much so I wouldn't end up in hell. Looking back on it now, I wish someone had told me the truth sooner. If only we had known that it was by *faith* in God's promise and the redemptive work of the cross, not our own "religious efforts," that makes us righteous. When we are born again, no longer are we merely "separated sinners." Instead, we become the children of God, and we can have a real relationship with Him. Not only that but God also desires to fill us up to overflowing with the Holy Spirit to transform us and everyone around us. That's what began to happen to me after I had received the infilling of the Holy Spirit.

———

Shortly after this whole experience, a friend called me and told me she had a terrible case of parasites. Back in those days, they would actually give you poison right up to the point of death to kill the parasites…but hopefully not you. My friend had become extremely ill from the poison, and she wanted us to come to her house to pray. I was so new in the Spirit that I really had no idea how to pray for healing. I had never been exposed to it much either; since growing up, our church didn't really believe in healing. It was quite backwards to think that the very thing that brought the salvation of many souls in the Bible supposedly no longer happened even though there are still many souls in each generation that need to be saved, but none of those old absurd beliefs mattered now that I was filled with the Spirit.

When we arrived at her house, she said to me, "The prayer of a righteous man avails much."

I honestly thought, *Who did she invite?*

My mind hadn't been renewed yet; I had no idea that I was now righteous because of Christ. I started to look around, thinking someone else was here to pray for her. Then I realized she was speaking about me.

I kept thinking to myself, *Really? Me? Righteous? I feel far from righteous.*

In reality, it didn't matter how I felt. What matters is the truth, which is God's Word. You see, she understood the verse in 2 Corinthians 5:21 (NIV) that says: "God made him who had no sin to be sin for us, so that in him we might become the righteousness of God."

She knew that our righteousness lies not in our own ability but rather in Jesus Christ, who now dwells in us. Therefore, we have now become the righteousness of God, and our prayers do avail much! For the first time in my life, I personally experienced the power of this revelation. When I prayed for her, she was completely healed. That miracle became the first of many. Time and time again, I have witnessed how the prayers of the righteous do indeed avail much.

The power of Christ now lives in us. What part of Jesus don't we have?

———

As I began witnessing healings, I also received the gift of seeing in the spiritual realm. I didn't really like it because I started to see demons. That was no fun. They were down-right ugly to look at. I kept insisting in prayer that I didn't want to see that, but later, I regretted asking God to take away the gift because I realized there are many people who need those who can discern what's going on in the spirit. God had gifted me with that in order to set people free, but I didn't understand that at the time.

One day, my sister-in-law brought her baby over to our house. The poor child had severely bent cleft feet. She laid him on our kitchen table, and instantly, I started to see in the spirit. I saw two snakes, one around each leg.

I said, "You foul spirit, get off that baby!"

Instantly, his feet straightened out in front of our eyes. God delivered him, and he never had a problem again. This is why it is important to be filled with the Holy Spirit. People need what we carry—the very power of God. This power can fill you with inexpressible joy, it can reverse the effects of poison, and it can set crooked feet straight. If you have not yet been filled, find someone to pray for you to receive the Holy Spirit today. What are you waiting for?

AUTHOR'S NOTES:

When Jesus was born, the angel of the Lord immediately announced the good news of His birth to the shepherds. Luke recounts that the angel said that this news will bring great *seriousness* to all people…just kidding. It says that this news "will bring great *joy* to all people" (Luke 2:10, NLT, emphasis added). When the Messiah came, it brought great joy! When we draw near to Jesus, it brings great joy! When He fills us up with His Spirit, it brings great joy! Why? Because part of the fruit of the Holy Spirit that is produced within us is joy.

"But the Holy Spirit produces this kind of fruit in our lives: love, joy, peace, patience, kindness, goodness, faithfulness, gentleness, and self-control."

GALATIANS 5:22–23A (NLT)

One of my favorite phrases in life is: "Seriousness is not a fruit of the Spirit, but joy is!" That isn't to say that there cannot be serious moments, but I believe God really is a joyful God! Sometimes, in our "religious fervor," we forget that He is the God who created laughter, jokes, and smiles. Like any good father, He wants to see His kids beaming with joy.

When I was hanging out with my elderly extended relatives while collecting stories for this book, I remember how happy they all were just sitting there. They were overcome with joy as they would recount the goodness of God in their lives. With each Holy Spirit–filled believer that I meet, I notice they carry a distinct joy within them. Whether it is expressed in a big and loud way or in a quiet reassurance, I can just feel it. I believe Christians should be the happiest people on the planet because we ought to be Christlike! If Christ is joyful, shouldn't we be?

CHAPTER 4
FLYING CARS IN 1974

My husband and I decided to spend the weekend at a Christian couple's retreat in northern Minnesota. We arrived in town on a Friday night, eager to spend some time with fellow believers. We headed over to the nearby restaurant, where some of the retreaters were visiting with one another before the event. It was a wonderful time meeting the other couples while sipping freshly brewed coffee and eating lots of goodies.

After a sweet time of fellowship, we returned to the retreat center quite late, hoping to get some sleep. I was surprised when the host of the event approached me to ask if I could do the devotional the next morning. The woman scheduled to lead the devotional for the retreat had to return home because her kids were sick, and someone had suggested that I could do it. The very mention of the idea shocked me. Speaking in front of a crowd did not come naturally to me. I grew anxious simply thinking about it.

He tried to reassure me by saying, "I know you have no time to prepare, so you can just read a Scripture and say a prayer," but he was adamant that he wanted me to do it. I finally conceded to his plea and agreed to lead the devotional the next morning.

As I walked back to my room, instant regret began to wash over me as I recalled how many qualified professionals were here at this very conference: knowledgeable teachers, skilled doctors, and accomplished executives. The more I thought about it, the more underqualified I felt. *How could I possibly have something impactful to share with them? How could I have agreed to share in front of such a large group of people on short notice? What was I going to say?* My thoughts were searching for any escape from this commitment.

Finally, a clever idea popped into my head. This seemed like the perfect moment to pull the 'submit to your husband' card. Surely, he would say there's no way I can do this, and I would be freed from this situation at last. Confident in finding my loophole, I remarked to him how they wanted me to lead the devotional in the morning, but with little time to prepare, I didn't see how I could ever possibly do it.

To my surprise, he looked at me and simply said, "Well, that's between you and the Lord." He then crawled into bed and went to sleep peacefully.

My witty idea had backfired, and I was still stuck with this responsibility. How was I going to get out of it now? As I sat on the edge of the bed in a cold sweat, my heart sank back into panic.

I cried out to the Lord, "I can't do this. I don't even know what I would say. I don't know what Scripture I would read." Instantly, He brought a Scripture to mind:

"Be thankful in all circumstances, for this is God's will for you who belong to Christ Jesus."

1 THESSALONIANS 5:18 NLT

He then impressed me to share about the time I had been severely burned and how He healed me. Even though I was still terrified to speak in front of people, I began to sense that God wanted me to do this. I wrestled within myself, struggling between what I now sensed God asking me to do and my own fears. The only way I could coax myself to sleep was thinking I would simply catch the MC in the morning and tell him I could not do it.

When I finally drifted off to sleep, I dreamt of speaking in the morning. The entire night, I saw myself sharing what God had shown me. When I woke up, I could still sense that God wanted me to speak, but despite what I felt in my spirit, my fear was determined to go tell the MC I could not do it. When we arrived at the center, I frantically searched for him, but he was nowhere to be found.

I continued to look until I heard my fears coming true over the microphone: "Now, Phyllis is going to do the devotional this morning. She has had no time to prepare; I just told her last night. So let's give her some grace."

It was too late now; I had to get up and do it. I approached the podium, trembling inside, and began to speak:

"When I was at a Bible study, someone had accidentally bumped a thirty-cup coffee maker near me. It ended up tumbling over, and all the boiling hot coffee poured onto my legs. I remember feeling the searing heat hit my knees and run down my legs all the way into my shoes. The instantaneous pain I felt was absolutely excruciating.

The bottom half of my legs and the top of my feet hurt so bad I could hardly stand it.

"In the midst of that horrible pain, Corrie Ten Boom's book, *The Hiding Place*, came to my mind. I remembered how Corrie's sister, Betsie, would say, 'In everything, give thanks.' It amazed me how Betsie even gave thanks when their own prison was infested with fleas. They would thank God for the fleas because it allowed them to have Bible studies in their cells since the guards did not want to be anywhere near the outbreak of pests.

"The story in Acts 16:25–26 recounts how Paul and Silas praised the Lord and gave thanks despite their circumstances in prison. Even though they were locked behind iron doors, that did not stop their praise, and I decided I wasn't going to let this pain stop my thanksgiving either. Although I could still feel my skin searing under the heat, I began to thank the Lord. I walked over to the sink and doused my aching legs with cold water. I could hear the hostess call the hospital frantically, asking what we should do. They told her to pack my legs with ice and bring me in to have the burns examined.

"When we arrived at the hospital, they brought me back to a room with a big basin of soapy water. I felt overwhelmed with dread when I realized they were going to scrub my blister-filled legs. Each tender blister broke against the harsh bristles of the brush running up and down my skin. I squeezed my eyes shut and kept uttering under my breath, 'Lord, I praise You. Lord, I thank You.' It took everything in me to turn my attention to the Lord instead of my pain. With each thanksgiving, the pain slowly became bearable. Finally, the scrubbing ceased, and they gently wrapped the wounds and sent me home.

"I remember lying in my bed that night, all propped up

on pillows. Every time my heart beat, it would hurt. Tears continually wet my cheeks from the intense pain I felt, but I kept repeating, 'Well, I'm going to praise You anyways, Lord. Thank You, Lord. Thank You, Lord.'

"When I woke up, I realized I had slept the entire night. Then I realized something even more crazy; I could not feel any pain in my legs. In disbelief at my sudden recovery, I began to gently pat them to see if I could feel anything. I was shocked when I felt absolutely no pain. So, I pressed even harder, but there was still no pain at all.

"A few days later, I went to the doctor's office to have my legs checked. My family doctor unwrapped the bandages to assess the wounds. He was in more shock than I was when he saw my legs only had a few faint scars instead of raw festering blisters.

"Scratching his head, not knowing what to say, the doctor simply remarked, 'Well, maybe they thought it was worse than it actually was?'

"Knowing now that it was a miracle, I reminded him that the hospital assured me that there would be scarring for a long time from burns this severe, but seeing my legs now, he still could not wrap his mind around it.

"All my pain from the burns had completely left that first morning after the accident and it never returned. Within two weeks, the scars had completely cleared up. You would have never known I was burned if you looked at me now. God supernaturally healed me, and I learned in everything, give thanks!"

—After I finished speaking, the keynote speaker came up and started sharing. I was surprised to learn during his message that the theme of the retreat was "In everything give thanks." Every Scripture the Lord had given me to share that morning, the Lord had also given him to share.

Throughout the retreat, he continuously referred back to my testimony to the point where I was a little embarrassed. Although I didn't like all the attention, I could see that it was God's hand at work the whole time. He knew I was going to have to speak, and He told me exactly what I needed to say.

Even in the midst of our fear, God can move mightily through us if we choose to obey Him.

———

During one of the evenings, the retreat hosted a talent show. Various people took the stage to share their talents with the crowd. It was such a joy to watch each one perform. To my surprise, my husband stood up with his autoharp to perform next. I was shocked to see it, knowing he would never be naturally inclined to stand up in front of a crowd.

He told the retreaters, "I don't have the talents that you all have for singing, but God has been giving me songs. I want to sing a couple of them that He's been showing me."

Even though he did not have the most eloquent voice, his songs were anointed. God's glory filled the room as his voice filled the air in pure worship. It was a beautiful moment to watch him play the instrument boldly for the Lord even though inwardly he was afraid. When I asked him later what happened, he told me that he didn't want to do it, but the Lord had asked him to.

Even in the midst of our fear, God can move mightily through us if we choose to obey Him.

———

On the last night of the retreat, the MC opened up the floor for people to share testimonies of what God had been doing through their lives. Several people stood up to share, including my husband. He began sharing how God was moving in his workplace. His boss had recently accepted Jesus after sharing the good news, and his foreman had decided to return back to the Lord as well. They were now hosting Bible studies and praying together before they started work.

I knew it was not of his own volition that caused him to stand up and speak. That look in his eye told me that his timid personality didn't want to, but he did it anyway because the Lord had asked him to.

Even in the midst of our fear, God can move mightily through us if we choose to obey Him!

———

We made one last pitstop at the restaurant to see our new friends before heading home. After we finished visiting with them, we got in the car and headed around the first curve. All of a sudden, something strange started happening. I could not describe to you what I felt in that moment.

My husband turned to me and said, "What is going on?"

"I don't know," I remarked, still wondering myself.

I did not hear anything or see anything. It felt like time had stopped for a moment. After a few seconds, I could feel the car touch down as if it had been in the air. When we began looking around, we realized we had been supernaturally transported to the next town over. I guess God had decided to take us for a little joy ride. We had covered around ten miles in a few seconds. When we realized what had happened, we both broke out in hysterical, holy laughter. I had never seen my husband laugh so hard in his entire life. He threw his arms up in worship as the joy of the Lord overwhelmed him. I remember thinking, *How are we still on the road if he is not steering,* but the car was supernaturally driving itself, as if Jesus had taken ahold of the wheel…literally.

I heard a loud voice speak as we were laughing: "Obedience, obedience, obedience."

I knew immediately why God had said that. It was because we had obeyed the Lord three times that weekend despite our fears. I guarantee you—you will never regret obeying God. My life with God has been far more adventurous than it would have been without Him. Whoever said following God is boring?

AUTHOR'S NOTES:

I loved hearing this story growing up. My grandma would tell it with wonder in her eyes and laughter in her voice. It continually reminded me that anything is possible with God (even flying cars), but it also showed me the importance of obeying God despite our fears.

I remember the first time I ever began to share publicly about Jesus. I was terribly nervous and felt extremely underqualified to be evangelizing. A few team members and I repeatedly passed a woman sitting outside at a café while we were walking around the streets of a busy city. I could not help but notice her, almost as if her presence was superimposed compared to everyone else.

When I looked at her, I would think, *Her mom is sick, and they have a rocky relationship.* I wondered why the thought kept coming to me about someone I knew nothing about.

After the sixth time we passed her, my leader turned to us and said, "I feel God highlighting that woman over there. Does anybody have anything for her?"

I hesitantly shared what I kept thinking, but I didn't think it could really be from God. We walked over anyway, and I knelt beside her. I shared what had been gnawing at my thoughts, and instantly, her walls came down. It was exactly what was going on in her life. She began to cry and even tremble, under the power of God. Never before had I witnessed someone experience God in such a tangible way outside of church walls. God began to move in her heart, and she powerfully encountered the love of God that day.

I remember walking away from that moment thinking, *I never want my fear to stop someone else's God encounter.*

However, it was not an instantaneous process, although I wish it had been. Rather, it was a slow process of choosing to obey God over that hideously loud voice of fear inside of me. Eventually, the voice of fear grew quieter as I built my confidence in the Lord.

Whether you are sharing on the street or at a retreat, don't let fear stop you from obeying God. We may think we cannot do bold things if we are shy and timid, but that is simply not true. God commands all believers to obey Him regardless of what we might think we are capable of. The old restrictive mentalities of how we see ourselves must be laid down at the altar. It's time to step out of our comfort zone. If you are afraid to do something for God, then do it afraid, but always obey God no matter what the cost. Are you willing to sacrifice your comfort and fear for His glory?

CHAPTER 5
FUDGE OPENS THE DOOR, JESUS WALKS IN

When I was just a young girl, my father and I had a special tradition. He would say to me, "You make the fudge, and I'll make the popcorn."

Much later in my life, my father moved into a nursing home after he became blind. One day, my daughter-in-law happened to call me while I was about to go visit my dad.

While we were reminiscing about the past, she said, "Why don't you make some fudge and popcorn and take it to the nursing home for your dad."

As soon as she told me, I knew it was the perfect idea to cheer Dad up, but I had no idea that it was actually a *God idea*. Looking back on the story now, I can see how Jesus was working behind the scenes to win over someone's heart through fudge. Isn't it funny how God can use something as simple as chocolate to draw us to Him? The Bible does say, "Taste and see that the Lord is good…" (Psalm 34:8 NIV). I think the key word here is *taste*.

When I arrived at the nursing home, I saw my sister was there as well, visiting with Dad. We all sat at the table and enjoyed some homemade chocolate as we chatted. My dad always complained about his roommate, Wilbur. Every time we would see him, he would tell us how grumpy Wilbur was. Even after being together for months, they never got along.

While I was still visiting with Dad, I heard a still small voice in my spirit: "Go give Wilbur some fudge."

I didn't even know he was in the commons area, but I looked around the room, and sure enough, Wilbur was sitting all alone a few tables down. I grabbed some of the fudge and walked over. Since Dad was blind, he didn't even notice that I was gone because my sister kept the conversation going. I knew that if he found out that I was on my way to talk to his "foe" and give him some of our special fudge, he might try to stop me.

When I sat down with Wilbur and offered him some fudge, his eyes lit up with joyful surprise as if I had given him the most thoughtful gift. He was delighted to share some chocolate with me. I talked with him for about a minute, and then I left to go back to the table where my dad was sitting.

About five minutes later, the Lord spoke to me again: "Go share with Wilbur."

I had no idea what I was going to say, but I stood up immediately to go share anyway. On my short walk over, I briefly prayed, asking the Lord to give me the words to say.

When I sat down at his table again, I said, "Wilbur, do you know God really loves you?"

In total shock, he said, "He does?"

"Do you know that He sent Jesus to die for you?"

In the same shocked tone, he exclaimed, "He did?"

It was as if he had never heard the gospel in his entire

life, and I am not sure if he ever had before that point. I kept sharing the good news with him and during our conversation, I told him about how God writes our name in His Book of Life when we belong to Him.

With eyes wide open, staring at me, he said, "He does?"

It seemed like everything I shared with him was all new news to him. He was very interested in every detail I told him. I finally asked Wilbur if he would like his life to belong to Jesus and have his name written in His book.

With delightful enthusiasm, he said, "I sure would!"

We prayed together, and Wilbur gave his life to Christ that day. After we finished praying, his countenance totally changed, and he was beaming with joy.

―――――

After that day, I would ask Wilbur every time I saw him at the nursing home, "Wilbur, do you remember how much God loves you?"

With a giant smile on his face, he would say right back to me, "I sure do!"

You could tell how happy he was after giving his life to Jesus. I never did end up telling my dad what had happened that day, but I wondered if he noticed anything different about him.

About a month later, I casually asked my dad, "How are you getting along with your roommate, Wilbur?"

You could tell he was a bit perplexed as he relayed to me, "You know, something has happened to him. He is completely different."

I shared the story with my dad how Wilbur had given his life to the Lord. Being overwhelmed with both joy and sadness, tears streamed down his face. He was delighted to hear that Wilbur had embraced the arms of the Savior, but it grieved him to realize that he had never thought to share the gospel with him. Instead, he had only chosen to complain about him. Sometimes we forget that those who are the biggest "sores" in our lives are often the ones who need the love of Jesus the most.

AUTHOR'S NOTES:

I remember reading about the brutal murder of a young girl in New York City, which, unfortunately, is not uncommon. However, what was unusual about this case was that it was witnessed by thirty-eight neighbors, yet no one had called the police until it was over...why?

The reason no one picked up the phone to call the police was because everyone else thought everybody else was already doing something.

This "bystander effect" is costly and dangerous thinking, especially when lives are at stake.

It is not uncommon in the West to encounter a similar mindset within the church walls. It appears to have permeated a multitude of congregations like a paralyzing infection. What are the grave implications of our inaction? It seems as if we've adopted a false sense of security, thinking that there are other people "sharing the gospel" or that there are other people out on the "mission field," but that's not "my call."

The call is for all!

The fact is, there may be someone sitting a few feet away from you who has never heard about the love of God. If we stay in our quiet corners and leave people be because we presume that "surely, they've already heard the gospel at some point," then it raises the unsettling but essential question: Are there people gripped by the chains of death, slipping into the depths of darkness because of our assumptions?

Church, let it not be so.

CHAPTER 6
GOD KNOWS HOW TO SELL CHICKEN

I was working as a salesman at the time for a large food corporation in Minneapolis. I mainly worked in their major accounts department, landing large orders for their products. I was doing really well at their Minneapolis branch, so they decided to offer me an even better position in Chicago after one of their hotshot salesmen moved out, but I politely declined. Shortly after that, they tried to offer me a position in their North Carolina branch, but I also decided to decline that promotion. They had territories all over the United States, but I knew God was aligning my steps to be exactly where He needed me to be. My boss still couldn't figure out why I had turned down these opportunities to work in some of their best territories. Still perplexed by the situation, he came to my office to see me.

I simply told him, "It just wasn't right."

We chatted for a little while, and I tried to explain my reasoning to him, but I think he left my office more confused about my decision than when he came in.

Not long after that, they offered me a position down in Florida. However, that territory was not like the money-making regions of Chicago or North Carolina; it was the exact opposite. Florida was known as their disaster territory. The company was having such a hard time keeping business running down there that they were going to withdraw their holdings and shut down operations altogether. When the opportunity opened up to go, I agreed almost immediately since the Lord confirmed that these were the doors He was opening up for me.

Now I knew I had my boss really perplexed. He came to my office again, "Why did you say yes to going to Florida?"

"Because God told me to go."

He didn't say anything; he just laughed. He thought it was funny that I talked to God, but I knew God was leading my footsteps.

I told him, "But listen, boss, I'll be back in Minneapolis in two years."

He laughed again. "That will never happen! Our corporation doesn't transfer people like that! No way will we see you in two years. It won't happen."

I didn't argue with him; in fact, I didn't say a word. I knew what God had told me, and I knew anything was possible with Jesus.

We packed up our things, sold our house, and headed down to sunny Florida. The business down there was scarce at best, but I knew God would give me the wisdom I needed to make sales. When we honor God in our business dealings and involve Him in our day-to-day lives, it's incredible what can happen.

We recently acquired a chicken company because our supplier couldn't afford the feed bill for all the chickens. At the same time, one of our biggest competitors had quit selling chicken. This of course, opened up all sorts of opportunities to acquire new business.

Before every meeting with new potential customers, I would pray and ask God, "What should I sell them?"

We had a whole list of products, so I needed God's wisdom to reveal to me which ones to discuss in order to be an effective salesman. God knew exactly what the customer wanted! They would purchase everything the Lord had shown me to propose. In fact, it was working so well that my boss came down to visit me in Florida. He felt that he needed to come see me in person to know how I was bringing in all this new clientele.

When he met with me, he asked, "How are you getting all these new accounts?"

"Well, I'm praying and asking the Lord for them."

He laughed like he usually did at my God comments. "Oh! That's a good one!"

He thought I was merely joking, but that's the only answer I would give him. He went back to Minneapolis with no "real" answers in his mind as to why Florida was starting to become a success. I continued to ask God for new accounts, and God kept answering my prayers.

———

I had offered to take out one of my new potential customers for dinner to discuss business. When the waiter came around to ask what we would like to drink, I asked for orange juice. Everyone else at the table ordered alcohol.

"Don't you drink?" my potential client asked with a somewhat judgmental look.

I shook my head.

He never asked me why I chose to be sober. Instead, he condemned me for not drinking.

Criticizing, he said, "I will never buy your product. I don't buy from people that don't drink."

In moments like these, do we give in and compromise our values for some extra cash, or do we stay true to what we believe, no matter what others may think? I decided I was not going to touch a drop of alcohol just to win over another customer. God is with me, and I want to honor Him in everything I do, including my business dealings.

In Proverbs, it says:

"When the Lord is pleased with the decisions you've made, he activates grace to turn enemies into friends."

PROVERBS 16:7 TPT

This is exactly what ended up happening with this customer. He eventually became one of my best clients down in Florida and purchased a whole lot of chicken from me over the years. If you honor God's ways, then He will bless you immensely.

"One skilled in business discovers prosperity, but the one who trusts in God is blessed beyond belief!"

PROVERBS 16:20 TPT

———

Another important customer I had down in Florida always wanted me to take him out to lunch to discuss business. He was one of our larger accounts down in this territory since he owned quite a few restaurants in the area. His favorite place to go was this particular restaurant where women would walk around in sheer clothing, and they were naked underneath. Every time I had a meeting with him on my calendar, I would dread going. I hated that place. The atmosphere felt disgusting. Whenever we would meet at that restaurant, I would look at anything but the waitresses.

When our next meeting rolled around, I walked in to find him licking his lips at the bar over the women walking by. I sat down in the meantime until he was ready to come over. I kept my eyes fixed on the wall while I patiently waited for him.

"Sir, sir," a woman began saying to me in a rather demanding tone.

"Yes?" I asked while keeping my eyes fixed on the wall.

"Why aren't you looking at me?" she insisted.

I politely replied, "I don't care to, thank you."

She walked away, stunned by my reaction. Most men came to this restaurant just to look at the women, but I knew that looking at them would not be honoring God.

Apparently, my client overheard our conversation at the bar and took it to heart. After that, conviction began to stir in him, and we never went back to that restaurant. He still remained one of our best accounts throughout the years.

———

With business thriving more than ever down in Florida, my boss flew down again.

"Now, seriously, tell me. How are you getting all these new accounts?"

In a mere six months, I exceeded their financial benchmark in one of their worst territories. I hit the target in such a short period of time that it was unheard of throughout the whole company. My boss was now all ears to hear about the means of my success. He was determined to know what I was doing to bring in so much revenue.

I stuck with the same answer: "I told you. I'm asking God for the business, and He's giving it to me."

This time, he was not laughing. He was perplexed, trying to make sense of it.

All he said was, "Okay."

He flew back to Minneapolis, not knowing what to think of it all.

———

In the meantime, school season was around the corner, and I needed to find a school in Florida for my four school-aged children. At the time, my wife and I didn't like the public schools in our area much since their education system was not very good. We started attending a church, and they also happened to have a school. We inquired to see if they had any openings, but they had absolutely none. We were disappointed because we really wanted them to go to this school. The director put us on a waiting list, but he didn't offer us much hope that there would be any sort of openings. They had absolutely no more room for any additional students.

Shortly after we had been placed on the waiting list, the director called us and said one of the families at school had moved away, so they had two new openings. Then, right after that, another family moved as well, so they had another two openings. All four spots that had opened happened to be the very grades my school-aged kids were all in.

As we were filling out all the paperwork to enroll the kids, the director remarked, "I don't believe it! I tell you this never happens!"

He had never seen openings become available so quickly. The whole ordeal left him stunned. We ended up starting a Bible study with him and a few others from the school. It's amazing how God opened up the doors for each one of our kids to go to a good school.

————

While we were still living down in Florida, my parents decided to come visit us. One of the highlights of the trip was being able to take my dad sea fishing. This was the first time either of us had been out on the ocean in a boat. That day we both managed to catch two large fish. It truly was an unforgettable experience with the salty breeze in our hair and our freshly caught meal prepared for dinner that evening. Our captain gave us instructions on how to cook our trophies and what seasoning to add to enhance the flavor.

When we got back to the house, I started preparing dinner. I added the seasonings along with some lemon juice and, lastly, topped it off with butter. I placed it on a metal baking sheet and set it all in the oven to broil. As we sat around the table, the aroma of freshly cooked fish began to fill the house. Finally, the timer went off, and it was ready to eat. When I pulled the sheet out of the oven, I noticed it was all warped from the heat. As I was holding it, the whole pan snapped back into place from the sudden temperature difference. All of that hot grease from the fish began running over my arm. I knew this was an instant recipe for a serious burn. I stood there, dripping with the scorching liquid. All I could think to do in that moment was thank the Lord.

My entire family watched in astonishment with mixed expressions of shock and concern. Even though I should have been severely burned from the searing heat, I never even showed a sign that boiling grease had touched my skin. It truly was a miracle that I never even felt the slightest sting of pain from the incident. God had supernaturally protected me, and we all enjoyed the wonderful fish that night.

As time went on, I continued to bring in sales with the Lord's help. Whenever I attended meetings, I always wore my fish lapel.

One day, one of my clients asked, "What's that fish? Are you a fisherman?"

I smiled. "No, that's the symbol that the early Christians used to identify one another as believers in the Lord Jesus."

He said, "I knew what that was, but I wanted to see if you were brave enough to tell me."

Never be afraid to stand up for your faith! You never know who may be watching. In fact, my boss at the time had been keeping tabs on me. All this new business that I was bringing in still intrigued him. He flew to Florida after I landed my eleventh major account that year.

"Okay, you have eleven new accounts. Now tell me exactly what you did."

My answer once again remained the same. "I told you before, boss. I asked God for the business."

He wasn't laughing this time either. "You did what now?"

For the first time, it seemed as if he was actually taking my answer seriously and wanted to know more.

I simply replied again, "I'm asking God for the business."

"We have twenty-nine salesmen, and not one of them has sold a single account, not one! Would you be willing to pray for my salespeople?"

So, I did. Turns out, God is really good at selling chicken.

————

Just shy of two years later, the man who had replaced me in Minneapolis passed away. When I had worked at that branch a few years prior, I had acquired some major accounts, including the corporation's second-largest account for the entire country. They knew I was familiar with the area and an expert with the customers on that portfolio, which made me the perfect candidate for the newly opened position. So, they ended up transferring me back up to Minneapolis just as the Lord had told me they would two years ago.

As we were preparing to return, I began to seek the Lord in prayer because I wasn't sure where we would move to. Before we left for Florida, there was a beautiful house for sale across the street from where we lived at the time. We went to one of the showings and absolutely loved it, but of course, we couldn't buy it since we were moving out of state. Unsurprisingly, it was sold to someone else, and I never thought much about it until now. As I prayed, the Lord reminded me of that house we had looked at before we left. He told me that it was the one He wanted us to buy, but I had no idea how I was going to buy something that was not for sale. I kept praying about it, but every time I did, that's the one the Lord would bring to mind. I couldn't shake it. It was as if He had already picked it out for us. I decided to pray and fast for a week because I thought that it would take a miracle to buy a house that wasn't even on the market.

After that week, I contacted some friends who lived near the house we had in mind. I figured they may have a way to reach the gentleman who had purchased the home. Back then, everyone had little directories that listed all the streets in the area and the names of everyone who lived on those streets. She was able to find out that his name was Bill, and she passed along his phone number that was listed with the address. I called and introduced myself, but I didn't really know what I was going to say.

I decided to just go for it. "I looked at your house before we moved down to Florida, and I want to buy it."

Of course, I was not surprised when he replied, "My house is not for sale. We recently bought it, and we absolutely love it. We don't want to sell it."

I wasn't sure what to say back, so we kept talking for a while about different things until I finally asked him, "Well, Bill, if you were to sell the house, what would you ask for it?"

"Thirty thousand dollars."

"Okay, I'll take it."

He paused momentarily, clearly stunned by my acceptance of his price—especially since he had just told me that his house was not for sale.

"No, my wife loves this house. We don't want to sell it. It is not for sale."

Once again, I didn't know what to do. We went back to talking about other things.

As we were about to wrap up our phone conversation, he said, "Okay, I'll sell it to you."

I was in shock, especially because this time I hadn't even asked. Of course, I agreed to buy it, and we packed up our things to move to Minnesota.

I still remember walking up to that stunning home on a cold November day. It felt particularly cold after coming from the sunny weather. Bill and his wife welcomed us in with coffee and rolls. We walked around the house and then visited with them for a while in the living room.

While we were talking, I asked Bill, "Why did you sell this house to us?"

He thought to himself momentarily and then said, "I honestly don't know. I just knew I had to."

I knew there was no way Bill would have ever sold us that house simply by asking. Without a doubt, God opened the doors for us to purchase that home. I thought it was because I had fasted and prayed, but later, God told me, "I would have given you that house even if you had not fasted one meal." It was simply God's kindness that allowed us to move into a house that we really loved. Living there was such a precious season of life for us because we absolutely cherished that God-given house. He really was with us every step of the way, from helping me land new accounts to getting our kids into a great school and even providing a beautiful home for us to come back to. If you seek Him in all you do, He will greatly bless you!

AUTHOR'S NOTES:

I used to believe the *only* way God wanted to connect with me was through something like prayer or worship. It wasn't until later in my walk with Jesus that He began to show me how much He cares about *every* detail of my life. No matter how ordinary or unimportant it might seem, God wants to be involved in all of it. Whether it's your workplace, your family, or even a purchase, God loves when we include Him in the process. Is there an area of life you could invite God into that you might not have thought about asking for His help before?

> "Trust in the Lord with all your heart and lean not on your own understanding; in all your ways submit to him, and he will make your paths straight."

> PROVERBS 3:5–6 NIV

Notice how it says, in *all* your ways—all happens to mean all. That includes everything: strengths and weaknesses, big and small, ordinary and extraordinary, natural and supernatural.

God told me once that true dependence on God is not just relying on Him when we can't do something but rather when we are perfectly capable of doing something and we still choose to rely on Him anyway.

You may be good at business or could figure out where to live all on your own, but when we choose to seek God in our weaknesses *and* our strengths, that is when we are truly submitting all our ways to Him.

Another reason I love this story is that no matter what, he never compromised his values, even if it upset his clients. Don't be afraid of what people may think of you when you stand up for righteousness; most of the time, the world is thinking wrong anyway.

> "But everyone who denies me here on earth, I will also deny before my Father in heaven."

MATTHEW 10:33 NLT

It's time as men and women of God to stand up for what we believe in, whether it be in our workplaces, schools, or neighborhoods; people will eventually see the fruit of what it looks like to follow God if we choose to walk in His ways.

CHAPTER 7
THROW A PARTY, ERVIN JUST GOT SAVED!

When I was a small boy, around two years old, I contracted double pneumonia. I was extremely ill, almost to the brink of death. We were living in a very small community at the time; it was around the early 1920s. There were about a hundred people in our town. Since we were out in the middle of nowhere in Iowa, everybody knew everybody in the community. There was nothing special about our town. We were mostly all farming families. It was quite rare to have any visitors passing through.

As I grew worse, my parents were left with little hope of my recovery until they heard a knock on the door. They were surprised when they saw a woman standing there who they had never seen before.

She told them, "I heard you have a son who is very ill. I've come here to help him."

Although she was a total stranger, they graciously welcomed her into the house. They were desperate for any sort of help for their son. She had an air about her that was different. Her mannerisms and accent made it seem as if she were foreign. She came into the room where I was bedridden and barely breathing. She simply placed an ointment over my chest and then left. I immediately started to turn around, and in a few days, I was up and running again like a normal little tot. When they told people around town what had happened, everyone was shocked because no one had ever seen or heard of the woman—before or since.

———

Although my health had miraculously turned around when I was young that didn't stop me from getting into all sorts of mischief. I remember when I was about twelve years old, my next-door neighbor hired me to catch gophers. They were always messing up his yard, and it drove him nuts. He agreed to pay me five cents for every gopher head I showed him, but I eventually got the idea to keep bringing him the same head. I thought I was such a clever little boy for racking up some extra change by cheating the old man. I had no sense of conviction over my actions until I got confirmed at the Lutheran church. I remember feeling something happen to me that day. It was as if my eyes were opened, and I had suddenly felt sorry for all the wrong I had done.

After the service, I confessed to my dad that I had been stealing from our neighbor. I thought he would be livid with me, but he didn't seem all that mad. Telling the truth wasn't as scary as I thought after all. All he said was that I should return the money and apologize for what I had done. That's what I felt led to do too. When we arrived back at the house, I gathered all the extra change I had collected from him. My dad and I walked over to the neighbor's house and returned the money. I knew deep down inside that it was the right thing to do.

After I was confirmed, there was a love in my heart for Jesus, but as time went on, my passion for God waned while other things began to pique my interest. My older brothers started partying, and it wasn't long before I followed in their footsteps. I got caught up in the thrill of it all. We loved to go out and have a good time. We would drink, smoke, and dance the night away. As I chased after the pleasures of what life had to offer, I began to completely forget about God, but He never forgot about me.

Looking back on my life, I can see how He continually protected me from death time and time again. There were several times I should have died or been seriously injured. One time, while I was driving toward a train track, I noticed a train was coming. I pressed on my brakes to stop the car and let the train pass by first, but I quickly realized there was a problem. My breaks had gone out—I couldn't stop. The roar of the approaching train filled my ears as it sped closer. I knew I was bound to be hit, yet somehow I wasn't.

Then I had another accident when I drove off a bridge, but I remained unscathed from the whole ordeal. There was also an incident where I had reached down for a map that was lying on the floor of my car. I lost control of my steering, and my car went rolling into the field. The vehicle landed upside down, completely battered all around by the damage of the tumble. Many onlookers did not even bother to see if I was okay because they figured I had died after taking one look at the wreckage. Yet I climbed out unharmed.

The accident that shook me up the worst was the morning I woke up at the depot near my house on the bench. I felt a slight breeze through my pocket and realized there was a hole from some burned-away fabric. The memory from last night was all a blur.

While I was still gaining consciousness, someone walked past me, chuckling. "I wonder whose car that is all burned up."

My heart sank as I put together the pieces of last night. I started to remember how I was totally drunk and decided to smoke a cigarette in my dad's mohair-interior car. From all the alcohol, I fell asleep in the vehicle while the cigarette in my hand drifted onto the short, furry upholstery, setting the car ablaze.

I vaguely remember someone pulling me out of the car, but I didn't know who it was. Who in their right mind would pull me out of a burning vehicle? How could I have only been left with a small hole in my pants after being engulfed in flames? The whole experience troubled me. I couldn't shake it. Something gnawed at me now.

A few weeks later, I was on my way to another party, but I didn't know why.

On the drive I started to ask myself, *What am I doing? What is all this for? Did it have any meaning? Is this how I would really spend the rest of my life? Is this all there is to it? I'll probably die soon if I keep living this way.* I pulled off on the side of the road and sat there. *Could this really be all that there is?*

This aching feeling of hopelessness swept over me. I started to drown in the fear of my own thoughts. I felt like somehow this was my last chance—the last glimmer of hope that mercy would offer me.

Then, I remembered that my sister had a powerful experience with the Lord. She began to pursue God after having a child out of wedlock. Being known for that kind of promiscuity back in those days meant having shame hurled on you from the community. Unable to cope under the weight of guilt, she turned to Jesus for help. When she accepted the Lord's forgiveness, waves of love washed over her. The Lord had redeemed her. Since that time, I could see that those who are forgiven much, love much. I knew that she was still serving God wholeheartedly, and I could turn to her in my desperate time of need. I knew she would not turn me away. I whipped the car around and headed for her house.

It was 3 am when I knocked on their door and shouted, "Edith, it's me, Ervin! I need to talk to you! I need Jesus!"

I'm sure they thought I was drunk or crazy or both, but when I got inside, they saw the hunger in my eyes. I was hungry for the Word of God—for the Bread of Life.

I remember her husband bringing out a large Bible and starting to read different Scriptures to me. I don't even know what he read because I was consumed by this urgency that I needed to give my life fully over to Jesus. I wanted him to pray for me so badly. Finally, we went through the sinner's prayer, and I surrendered my life to Jesus as my Lord and Savior.

The next morning, I went out to my car and dumped out all my beer and whiskey bottles. There was no turning back to that lifestyle now. I was all in. I stayed with my sister for about a week so that I could keep learning about Jesus. When we are young in the Lord, we need good Godly company.

When I arrived back home, I found the house was packed with people. My family had invited some people over from church and decided to throw a party for me to celebrate my salvation since I was the *last* person they thought would come to Christ. Practically the whole town had heard that I had given my life to Jesus. Everybody kept remarking that they were hoping for the young people to get saved, but they never thought it would be Ervin.

AUTHOR'S NOTES:

God really does desire that none should perish (see 2 Peter 3:9). I believe it was God's mercy that continually saved him from death because Jesus desired for Ervin to live in His Kingdom. God had a plan and purpose for his life, but the enemy tries to do everything he can to distract us from what God has for us. Yet, God's mercy continually rescues us from our own foolish ways. He wants us to be set free from our lifestyles that are only leading us to death, but God knows it is ultimately our choice since He has given us free will. The choice we make will not only affect our own life but also the lives of everyone around us.

Ervin was my grandpa. When he chose to repent and leave his lifestyle behind, it would ultimately shape generations to come. If he had continued in his ways, he may have raised a family that only knew a lifestyle of being held captive to the world's desires. Instead, he was able to leave behind a legacy of righteousness and freedom in Christ. All his days, Ervin served the Lord. He was a faithful man who followed Jesus with all his heart. His life has been and is a huge inspiration to me. It is one thing to start strong in the Lord; it is an entirely different matter to remain steadfast to Him until your dying breath.

CHAPTER 8
CAN PRAYER CHANGE GOD'S MIND?

This is the story of where it all began for the Welches and Lyles. This is how the Lord broke through the family line and rescued us out of darkness.

––––––

The Welch family would invite us, the Lyles, over to their house on the weekend to party with them. The Welches were very musically talented. Their remarkable gift filled the atmosphere with lively music as we danced the night away. We had so much fun. We would get drunk and enjoy all the pleasures that life had to offer. That's all we knew to do; we didn't know there was anything else to life except for these fleeting moments of enjoyment that always left us empty and wanting more.

Since we frequently spent time with the Welches, I—Lillian Lyle—became well acquainted with Mr. Leo Welch. It wasn't long before I married him. We spent the early years of marriage still partying and drinking like we usually had. We were completely clueless when it came to Jesus. None of the Welches or Lyles had ever heard a thing about the gospel until I saw that someone was coming to our small town to hold some sort of tent meeting. Since there was never much to do around here, I decided to go, not having the faintest idea what to expect.

As I sat there listening to the evangelist, it was like music to my ears. A sweetness filled my soul. It was absolutely the most wonderful news I had ever heard in my entire life. When he gave an altar call to become born again, I immediately went forward to give my life to Jesus. When I went home that night, I told Leo all about it. I couldn't stop talking about this Jesus. Everywhere I went, I started inviting people to the meeting.

The next day, Leo and I went to the tent. Leo was convicted when he heard the message, but he didn't go forward when the preacher gave the altar call. He had wanted to go forward, but his fear held him back. That night, when we arrived back at our home, he was restless. He was flooded with regret over the fact that he hadn't prayed to receive Jesus. The next day, he went to the meeting again and immediately gave his life to the Lord.

I started to tell all the Lyles and Welches about Jesus. I just couldn't help it! I knew they had to go hear this preacher and get saved. Slowly, one by one, my family and friends started to come to the meeting to hear about the wonderful news of Jesus and surrender their lives to Him. After a while, our parties ceased. Once we were offered true joy, we didn't want to go back to our old lifestyles.

I knew my parents had to hear about this Jesus too, but traveling twenty-three miles in the country to go visit them was a lot more difficult in the early 1930s than it is today.

We finally made the trip out to my parents' farm, and I told my dad, "You have to come and hear this preacher!"

He tried to brush it aside by saying, "I can't come. I got too much to do here on the farm."

Despite his resistance, I kept urging him to come with me because I knew this was far more important than ol' farm chores. Finally, he gave in to my protest and came with me to the tent meeting. When the evangelist gave the altar call, he immediately went forward.

All of a sudden, he started jumping up and down. He exclaimed with joy, "I've got it! I've got it! I've got it!"

He was such a happy man after he received Jesus into his heart. He was so happy in fact, that he quit drinking. Dad used to get drunk a lot, and it drove our mother nuts. Now everything about him was changing. When he returned back home to the farm, Mom could see a noticeable difference. When I pressed her to go to the tent meeting, she tried to assure me that she didn't need to be saved because she was already a "good enough" person. Thankfully, this deceptive thinking didn't last forever. Eventually, my mom gave her life to Jesus too.

A few months after my dad was born again, I went out to visit him.

"Lillian, I'm just so happy! So happy! I wish I could go right straight up to Jesus!" he said, smiling at the heavens.

The next day, he fell over dead. His heart's desire came to pass, and he went home to be with the Lord.

———

As time went on, Leo and I continued to serve the Lord and raise our family. Taking care of eight kids wasn't easy, especially with a faulty heart. My symptoms seem to be growing worse by the year. Since I was young, I was told that something in my heart wasn't right, but now it felt like every day was a fight for life. During these months, I remember sitting in my bedroom one day and looking out the window. A songbird flew over and landed right near me on the other side of the glass. It was the dead of winter in the Midwest, so it was unusual to be seeing that kind of bird in the first place. Then the bird started to sing to me, which made the whole situation even more peculiar.

The Lord spoke to me clear as day, "Get your house in order because you'll be coming home in the spring."

I prayed for seven days and seven nights straight. I told the Lord over and over, "I can't come home yet. No one will ever pray for my kids the way I will. Please let me stay."

At the end of the seven days, the Lord gave me the Scripture in Isaiah 38:5, where the prophet tells Hezekiah that God had heard his prayer and would add fifteen years to his life. This verse was exactly the confirmation I needed. I knew that God had heard my prayer, and I was going to live. I had this assurance, but while I was pregnant with my ninth child in my early forties, my heart began to fail me.

During the pregnancy, I also contracted pneumonia. The combination of everything was too much for my body, and I ended up losing my child. My health was now rapidly declining, and I was left with little hope of survival. Back in the 1950s, heart surgery was still in its experimental stages. When I considered it as an option, they told me my life expectancy would only be around an additional seven years. They were trying a new kind of heart surgery at that time for patients with my condition. Instead of splitting open the breastbone, they cut underneath the arm. The surgeon would then reach in with a knife on his finger and trim away the damaged tissue just by the feeling—talk about an experiment indeed.

I decided to take the risk and have the surgery. After the operation, I was still in the hospital for months recovering. Out of the six people who had this type of operation, I was the only one who survived. I knew God had given me a word that He would sustain my life, but it seemed like I wasn't getting better. There were multiple times that the hospital would call my family in to say goodbye because they didn't think I would live much longer. After several months of a rocky recovery, my husband started to lose hope.

He went down to the woods to pray, and while he was there, God spoke to him, "Your wife will be healed, and she will come home."

After seeing his wife fight to live for weeks, he didn't really believe it, so God spoke to him a second time, "She will be healed, and she will come home."

He still struggled to believe that his wife would return, so the Lord spoke a third time, in a loud, if not audible, voice, "She will be healed, and she will come home!"

Then, it finally hit him that God will heal his wife! He started telling everyone that I was coming home. Most of them thought he had lost his mind, including the doctors. He took me out of the hospital, but it was too soon. I started to get weaker and weaker at home, almost to the brink of death. Of course, the doctors were upset when he had taken me out, but a few weeks later, they called and graciously offered to have an ambulance take me back to see if there was anything else they could do to help my recovery. I went back to the hospital, but not much seemed to change.

One evening, when they almost thought they were losing me again, my family went down to the church to pray for me. Immediately, my strength started returning. It felt as if life was flowing through my veins.

About a week later, the doctors said, "You can go home now. It seems that there's nothing more we can do for you. You're healed."

As I got up and walked out of the hospital, I saw about thirty nurses and doctors lining the hallway. With tears streaming down their faces, they watched as I walked down the hall. They saw how I struggled to fight for life for months, but they knew God had restored my health. It was an emotional moment to release someone to go home who they didn't think would make it, but God turned it all around. I was finally able to go home and raise my family.

———

After fifteen years had passed, my health took a sudden turn for the worse. I thought maybe that my time was up. The verse God had given me in prayer clearly stated that He added *fifteen* years to Hezekiah's life. After going through some testing, they found that one of my valves needed to be replaced. The doctors suggested another surgery. Although the technology had advanced over the years, this was still a very risky surgery.

I was prepared to go home to be with Jesus when I went into the operation, but I woke up from the medical procedure feeling completely fine. I thought maybe I would pass on to be with the Lord while I was recovering, but I didn't. In fact, another fifteen years came and went. I guess the Lord had given me more than fifteen years. Now I was up to thirty.

The doctors continually considered me a miracle. Every once in a while, they wanted me to come into the university to examine me. After all, for them, I had made medical history by being one of the earliest and oldest survivors of open-heart surgery at the Minneapolis Heart Institute. A large room full of whitecoats would all be studying me in great detail. I didn't like all the attention very much. I was grateful that they helped fix the issues going on in my heart, but I knew the real reason I had survived was because of God.

———

Another three years had passed by, and I was trudging through the snow on a frigid winter day. The snow was deep, and the air was bitterly cold. I could feel something was wrong, but I didn't know what. They took me to the hospital, and the doctors told me that the stitching had been damaged from my second surgery. I decided to go through a third operation, but this time I was ready to go home to be with Jesus. They attempted to restitch the valve, but while I was recovering, I felt like my mission was complete.

In my last days, the Lord spoke to me Daniel 12:3 (NIV), "Those who are wise will shine like the brightness of the heavens, and those who lead many to righteousness, like the stars for ever and ever." He continued, "And you will shine as the stars in heaven."

Tears streamed down my face. I didn't understand; I felt like I hadn't really led anyone to righteousness, but God wasn't looking at the "numbers." He was looking at all those conversations I had with my friends and family where I couldn't shut up about Jesus. He knew all the seeds I planted would one day grow up to be a strong harvest that would last five generations and beyond.

I lived a total of thirty-three years past what the Lord had originally told me. He changed His mind and answered my prayer. He knew that I wanted more time on earth to take care of my kids and intercede for them. When He answered my prayer, He didn't give me the fifteen years that He had given Hezekiah; He gave me the thirty-three years of His own life. All that time, it was *His* very life that sustained me.

AUTHOR'S NOTES:

You never know how one small act of obedience could change generations to come. The tent evangelist who came to the countryside probably had no idea of the ripple effect he created in our family. That little mustard seed of faith that was planted in Lillian's heart grew in good soil and reaped much more than had been planted (see Matthew 13:3–8). Her salvation ultimately led to the salvation of many others in our family, including future generations like me.

God told me once that He can always work with a seed. What a mighty thing a seed can become in the hands of the Lord! If we are faithful to plant, God will bring the increase (see 1 Corinthians 3:6–7). Every time you share the gospel, it changes something, whether you see the results of it or not. Even if we don't see the impact, what we do matters and so do our prayers. God is sovereign, but He is also relational. Our prayers *can* change things, even God's mind.

CHAPTER 9
THE WHEELS ON THE BUS GO ROUND AND ROUND

I had heard that one of my friends, Dave, recently purchased a school bus company. I decided to give him a call to see if he needed any more drivers since I was looking for work after moving back to the cities. The next thing you know, I was off to take my bus driver's test in order to get my commercial driving license for the job. It truly was a miracle because I had never driven a bus before in my life, but I was able to complete everything my instructor asked me to do with ease. Once I passed the test, I got the job. God was opening the doors for me all along the way.

My very first route was for a school that was dedicated to providing education for kids with special needs, but like any other school bus, there were always some bullies along for the ride. The meanest kid on my bus was named Johnny. One day, he decided he would wait for the other kids to get off the bus while sitting sideways on his seat. As the other kids passed by, he would kick them into the seat across the aisleway. I watched for a moment, as one by one, kids started falling when they tried to walk by his seat. The instinctual protective dad in me compelled me to action. I put the brakes on and walked back to where Johnny was.

I tried to confront him, but it only grew worse. Johnny was causing a lot of issues, but God used the whole situation to allow me to become better acquainted with the school leadership. We ended up starting a wonderful Bible study at the school on Tuesday nights. Many of the children from school joined our meeting, and God began to move in the hearts of many of the kids during our time studying the Word.

———

In the meantime, Johnny's caretaker designed a poker-chip system to try to subside his mischief. Every time he got on the bus, he would give it to me. If he was good that day, I would give it back to him, but if he misbehaved, then I would keep the chip. If he did not return home with the poker chip, then he would lose his TV privileges.

He also had to start sitting on the seat behind me so I could keep an eye on him. Shortly after he had been bumped up to "first class," I started sharing the gospel with him since he was now within earshot. After talking for a while, I asked if he would like to be born again. That day Johnny decided to surrender his life to Jesus upon hearing the good news. Right after he got off the bus, his right-hand "muscle man," Wayne, moved into the seat where Johnny had been sitting.

He said, "I want to do what Johnny just did."

I shared the gospel with Wayne, and he also gave his life to Jesus. They were the first two kids on my bus to get saved.

After that day, Johnny and Wayne were no longer the mean bullies they once were. God completely transformed them. In fact, the seat where they gave their lives to Christ became the "hot seat" on my bus. Johnny ended up moving to another seat because, each day, a different kid would sit there to hear the gospel. One by one, the kids surrendered their lives to Jesus.

————

As the kids were getting saved, more and more miracles began to happen. I remember on one occasion, one of the regular attendees of our Bible study had missed school that day because she was sick. I didn't expect her to be at the meeting that evening. You can imagine my surprise when I saw her walking down the hall on her way.

"They told me you were sick. What happened?"

"Well…I was lying in bed because I wasn't feeling good, but then the door opened to my room. It was Jesus, and He walked over to me."

Intrigued by her response, I asked, "Then what happened?"

"Well," she continued on innocently, "He said, 'I don't want you to have a sore throat anymore.' Then He put His hand on my neck, and I didn't have a sore throat anymore."

God had completely healed her. She was one of many who encountered Jesus in a powerful way.

————

The atmosphere of the bus began to change completely. There were thirty-three kids who rode on my bus, and throughout the weeks that followed, thirty-two of them had given their lives to Jesus. However, there was still one more God was after. She was particularly troubled. While she rode on the bus, she would take her shoes off and smell the inside of them. If anybody ever worked up the courage to sit near her, she would start beating them with her shoes. If there was no one to beat with her shoes, then she would start talking to a demon by name as she rode on the bus. Occasionally, I could overhear what she was saying as she carried on conversing with the demonic spirit out loud, just like she would with a friend. I knew she needed Jesus, but she wanted nothing to do with the revival that was happening on the bus.

Then the day came when God opened up the perfect opportunity to share the good news with her.

I had finished dropping off all the kids at school, and on my way back, I heard this little voice shout from behind, "Hey, bus driver!"

I remember thinking, *Oh shoot! Someone's still on the bus.*

Normally, after I drop the kids off, I walk up and down the aisle to make sure everybody has gotten off, but this time, I forgot to do my usual inspection.

I didn't know who it was, so I shouted back, "Who's on the bus?"

She got up and sat in the seat closest to me. It was that very little girl I had been wanting to share the gospel with. I knew that God had set this whole thing up.

"What are you doing on the bus?" I asked.

She didn't reply. Instead, she laid down on the seat and shut her eyes to try to go back to sleep. I immediately turned the bus around to take her to school.

While we were on our way, I asked, "Can I tell you about Jesus?"

"No!" she shouted.

Calmly, I asked again, "Can I tell you about Jesus?"

"No!" she persisted.

I said to myself, "Well, Lord, what can I do?"

He immediately showed me that this was not merely a matter of disinterest in hearing the gospel; rather, there were demonic forces at work that were trying to stop her from listening to the good news. The Lord instructed me on how to navigate this spiritual battle. I prayed under my breath, rebuking the demon, and then asked her again, "Can I tell you about Jesus?"

With a complete shift in her behavior, she said, "Yes."

After I finished sharing the gospel with her, I asked, "Wouldn't you like to ask Jesus to come into your heart?"

"No!"

I was surprised by her reply. Her demeanor seemed to go right back to what it was before I had prayed for this captive to be set free. I decided to share more about the love of God and His power to transform us when we decide to have a relationship with Him, but despite asking again, she still held firm to her answer.

I asked Jesus, "Lord, what do I do?"

He revealed to me once again that there was another spirit that was hindering her from receiving Jesus. I rebuked that demon as well and then asked her again if she'd like to be saved.

This time, she declared with certainty, "Yes, I would!"

At that very moment, I happened to be sitting at an intersection, and the traffic was so bad that I couldn't pull out onto the street for a very long time. I could clearly see that it was God setting the whole thing up. As we prayed, I also asked her if she would like to get rid of that foul spirit that she called by name all the time on the bus. She gladly agreed to renounce that malevolent spirit and I cast that demon out!

After that day, she never took off her shoes to smell them again, and she never hit another person. She quit talking to that foul spirit, and God completely transformed her demeanor.

Shortly after she gave her life to Jesus, I noticed she had not been on the bus for a few days. I finally asked her caretaker if she knew where she was.

She told me, "Oh, she moved away to a different city."

Saddened by the news, I asked the Lord, "Why did she go there?"

He said, "I sent her up here just so she could hear about My Son, and now she has."

She was the last one to get saved on my bus. It was a bittersweet moment to see her go. I cherished the time I had with each and every one of those kids. It was such a privilege to be able to share the gospel with all of them.

———

I ended up running into Johnny years later at a restaurant. The first words out of his mouth were, "I still love Jesus, and He's living in my heart."

AUTHOR'S NOTES:

Sharing the good news is spiritual warfare. There are demons at work that don't want people to hear and receive the gospel. As believers, we need to rebuke those meddling demons! God equips His soldiers with the power and authority needed as the gospel is preached. God gave believers authority to "… trample upon every demon before you and overcome every power Satan possesses" (see Luke 10:17–20 TPT). He gave us this authority so that we can free those who are bound by the power of the enemy. One of the ways we can exercise our authority is through prayer. When we engage in prayer alongside evangelism, it creates a powerful combination to help set captives free. Remember, we have the armor of God and the sword of the Spirit for a reason—not just to look like soldiers but to *be* soldiers. Now is the time to plunder hell and populate heaven!

CHAPTER 10
YOU'VE GOT MAIL!

I was living in Minnesota around the mid-1900s while my daughter lived down in Texas. We were close in heart, but the long distance made it difficult to stay in touch. We communicated mainly by letter back in those days. Phone calls were very expensive at the time since you had to pay by the minute to talk on the phone for long-distance calls.

I knew my daughter had been struggling with depression in that season of her life. One day, the Lord led me to write a letter to her. I sat down to write, and the words flowed out of me. I knew that the Holy Spirit was inspiring each word as if He were writing the letter Himself. I could sense it was exactly what she needed to hear.

I placed the letter in an envelope and addressed it to her. I headed out the door to go to the post office in town to buy a stamp to mail the letter. When I walked outside, the wind was so fierce that the letter blew away before I could even get to the car. It was caught up by the gust so fast that it disappeared out of sight in an instant. I knew there was no way I could catch it.

I walked into the house feeling defeated and disappointed, knowing there was no way I could re-create the letter I had just written. At the very least, I tried to sit down and write another, but this time the words did not flow. I wrote down what I could from memory, but I knew it was not the same. Regardless, I sealed it up and went down to the post office. I stuck a stamp on it and sent it off.

The next morning, I received a phone call from my daughter. She sounded absolutely ecstatic. It had been a long time since I had heard her sound joyful since she had been battling depression. I wondered what had happened.

She exclaimed over the phone, "I received your letter, Mom! It was exactly what I needed to hear! Thank you so much for sending it, but I was wondering how did it get here without a stamp on it?"

AUTHOR'S NOTES:

God's love for our loved ones greatly surpasses our own. He tenderly cares about each detail of our lives and the matters that are dear to our hearts, like our families. Stories like these leave me in awe and wonder when I think about how incredible it truly is to have a letter supernaturally transported across the country in less than a day just to encourage one of His kids in a difficult season. There truly is none like Him!

CHAPTER 11
FUN IN THE SUN

Our family headed down to Sanibel Island in Florida to get some sunshine in the middle of another cold northern winter. My husband and I had so much fun walking on the beach and collecting shells. Along with our adult kids, one of my son's friends had joined us on the trip. He was a bit of a clown and absolutely loved to make people laugh.

He knew how much I loved collecting shells, so he told me, "I'll go swim out in the ocean and get you some really pretty shells."

He made a whole scene out of it as he swam out and dove into the crystal-blue water. He would dig for a shell and then toss it to me along the shore. I laughed and laughed as he continued on. We were having such a fun time simply enjoying God's creation. I hadn't realized that nearby beachgoers had been watching the whole comical scene take place.

One lady strolling along approached me to ask, "Is that your son?"

I chuckled. "Oh, no. That's actually my son's friend who's here with us on our family vacation."

Curious, she asked, "You know we're about the same age, and it's sad that our kids just don't need us anymore like they used to. What do you do with all your time?"

"Well, I work a little...I play a little...and would you believe that sometimes I go around telling people how good God is and what He has done for me?"

"Well...what has He ever done for you?"

I smiled. "Do you have an hour or so?"

She nodded and I began sharing with her about how God had healed me and the many wonderful things God had done for me since then. She was hanging on every word as we walked along the shore.

After a short while, her husband walked over to where we were standing and started talking to his wife in Norwegian. He wanted to know what we had been discussing. My husband nearby overheard the familiarity of his native tongue being spoken, so he made his way over too and decided to join in on the conversation. Our husbands started chatting back and forth in Norwegian until eventually, we decided to let them talk together and carry on with our conversation instead.

They stood there laughing and talking as we made our way back down the shoreline. I continued to share about Jesus and then decided to ask my new friend if she wanted to receive Jesus into her life too.

She joyfully agreed and then remarked, "You know, it's funny because something has happened to my sisters. I didn't know what it was until today. They would always keep giving me books and tapes and different things about all this Christian stuff."

I asked, "Well, do you read the books they give you?"

She shook her head with a chuckle. "No."

"Have you listened to any of the tapes?"

She laughed again. "Well, no, not exactly."

I knew this whole conversation was God's way of finally drawing her heart to Him. So, I said, "Well, let's pray together then."

I led her through a prayer to surrender her life to Jesus and then I said, "Oh, you'll need the power of the Holy Spirit too."

I laid my hand on her head and said, "Be filled with the Holy Spirit!"

She shouted on the beach, "Wow! I felt that!"

She started marveling over everything that had happened. I think she was beginning to realize that this was God's hand at work all along.

She told me, "There is not one reason in the world I should come to Sanibel Island. I live on Hilton Head in South Carolina, and we are surrounded by water, but for some reason, I knew I had to come to Sanibel Island. In fact, I knew I had to come this very weekend, and now I know why."

I never saw her again after that, but I guarantee that her sisters had been praying for her salvation. It's funny how sometimes we are more willing to listen to strangers than we are to our own family, but either way, God knows how to coordinate the events of our lives to bring us to Him.

AUTHOR'S NOTES:

My favorite part of this story is that it simply started by having fun. People recognize true joy when they see it. The world is craving the Kingdom of joy, peace, and righteousness that we carry. The great news is we have the privilege of bringing the Kingdom wherever we go.

Whether we are on the mission field, at home, or even on vacation, there are always people who need to hear the wonderful news of Jesus. If you've never shared the gospel with anyone or don't know how, start by telling a testimony of God's goodness in your life. This is a great way to begin to share the truth of the gospel by talking about the effects of it in your own life. You have no idea how this might impact a person. Your testimony is powerful, and what's even more powerful is the presence of Jesus that lives inside of you.

When you overflow with God, people will be touched by the love of God as you share. Sometimes we can become too caught up in "having the right words" before we preach the gospel instead of focusing on the fact that people aren't hungry for good theology; they are hungry for true love. Of course, we should have solid theology as well, but what I am trying to convey is that people desire to *experience* the power of the gospel, not just learn about it.

Every person longs for the very qualities of God's nature: joy, peace, hope, and love. Hungry souls are drawn to those who walk in His likeness because they yearn for who God truly is. We may still do ordinary things like walk on the beach and be silly, but remember that you also carry the extraordinary treasure of the Kingdom that the world is searching for. Have fun preaching the gospel and preach the gospel while having fun!

CHAPTER 12
FAITH IS OUR FUEL, LITERALLY

We were in one of the most difficult seasons of our lives. Groceries were running low, and with lots of little mouths to feed, my wife and I wondered how we would make it with little to no money. There were moments when we felt absolutely destitute. I had been working for a man at the time, but he kept holding off on paying me. Weeks would go by without a single cent for my work.

It seemed to be a continual struggle for us. Some dear friends of ours invited us to come over to pray together about the matter. When we arrived at their house, we saw another couple sitting around the table as well. Internally, I was very upset. We were supposed to be here to pray with some close friends over a private matter, and here were strangers sitting at the table with us. I didn't know these people, and to be honest, being broke was not exactly news I wanted to share with just anyone. We visited with one another for a while over some good ol' ice cream.

Our friend would pass out small little spoons along with the dessert and say, "Ice cream is to be enjoyed in small bites."

I couldn't agree more.

After we got through eating, our friends said, "Now, let's pray about this ordeal."

Nevertheless, I still didn't feel like praying with this other couple that we didn't know. It didn't seem like I had much of a choice in the matter, so we began praying anyway.

This stranger turned to me and said, "God has been asking you to do something, and you will not do it. Why won't you do it?"

With that one statement, he hit the nail on the head. I was blown away by his ability to hear God's voice. I knew that God had arranged for this man to be here praying with us so that He could reach my heart. The truth was that the Lord had been asking me to do something that I had not done yet. It was a spiritual matter I had been putting off. As soon as I got home, I took care of it.

Shortly after this, the man who owed me all the money for my labor sent me a big check in the mail. Then it seemed like everyone we knew started to buy us groceries out of the blue. Pretty soon, our dining room table was full of a pile of food that different people had brought. The floodgates of blessing were opened because spiritual obedience can bring physical results.

———

Although we were starting to see the Lord's abundance be poured out, we were not through our valley yet. With eight kids, a pile of groceries can get used up quick and so can toilet paper. One day, we were almost out of that too. We had only a few pieces left on the roll, but we weren't out yet. One of my sisters had stopped by to visit, and when she left, I assumed she drove straight home. A short while later, I heard a knock at the door. She stood in the doorway holding a large bag in her hand.

"What's this?" I asked.

"Well, I was driving down the street, and the Lord told me to buy you toilet paper," she said as she handed me the bag.

Isn't it incredible how the Lord cares for us even when we go through a crappy situation?

———

We were still struggling for money, carefully dispersing every dollar that came in for our basic necessities. One of our friends had invited us to their daughter's wedding in downtown St. Paul. We made our way down to the cities and picked up a friend along the way who also needed a ride. After driving all those miles to the event, it was looking like we were going to run out of fuel.

When the wedding was finished, I tried to start the car to drive home, but it would not start. I saw the gas gauge was indeed on empty. I didn't even have enough gas to get to the gas station. Even if I did make it, I only had one dollar in my billfold. Back in the 1970s, you had to put a deposit down for the metal can in order to fill up your gas tank so I could not even get one dollar's worth of gas.

One of my friends, Ed, noticed we were just sitting there in our car. He came over and asked, "Is everything okay? Do you need any help?"

I wanted to tell him what was going on, but the Lord spoke very clearly to me to say to him, "No, everything's okay."

I did exactly as the Lord instructed, even though it

seemed counterintuitive to me. Ed got in his car and drove off. I tried to turn the engine on again, and this time, the car started. With no gas in the tank, we drove from downtown to my brother's house, which was about thirty miles away, west of the Twin Cities. It was an absolute miracle.

We visited with my brother's family until it was so late that the kids ended up falling asleep. My brother graciously invited us to stay the night. There were kids sleeping all over the place. When I was getting ready to go to bed, I prayed for the Lord to provide because I still needed gas to leave the house. I wasn't sure what we were going to do. While I was kneeling down, I heard a knock on the door.

My brother asked, "Do you need money?"

"I sure do," I said humbly.

He handed me a twenty-dollar bill. "Here, take this."

Back in those days, this was more than enough to get us home. It also allowed us to buy many more much-needed groceries. I was so grateful for my brother and my whole family. It moves me to tears to think how they helped us through this season. If it was not for Jesus and all my family, I'm sure there would have been many nights we could have gone hungry. Praise God! He always provides!

AUTHOR'S NOTES:

The Lord is our provider. No matter what we are going through, the Lord cares about every detail of our lives. There are times when God provides through people, if we are willing to receive. There are times when God provides opportunities, if we are willing to put in the effort. While there are other times when God supernaturally intervenes for us. No matter what, we trust in Him to provide for our every need.

CHAPTER 13
DEATH, THERE'S THE FRONT DOOR

I arrived back home after a tiring day at work. My husband wasn't inside so I walked out onto the deck to try to find him. He was outside doing some spring cleanup on our yard, but I noticed he was barely moving as he walked around picking up branches.

"Ervin, why are you working when you're so tired?" I shouted down. "Come inside and rest."

He came into the house and decided to lie down on the couch for a while, which was very uncharacteristic of him. Now I was starting to get worried.

I sat down beside him on the couch, "Are you okay?"

"I'm fine. I'm fine." He tried to reassure me, but I knew he always downplayed his symptoms.

He continued to recline on the couch and I kept walking over to check on him. Each time, he tried to reassure me that he was all right, but the way he looked wasn't convincing me.

After a little while, he walked over and sat at the dining table to eat the grilled cheese sandwich and tomato soup that I had made him. Normally, he prayed over the meal before eating, but this time, he just sat there in silence.

"Were you going to pray?" I asked, but he never answered me.

I decided I would pray over the meal instead and for his health as well. When I finished praying, he didn't say a word. He picked up his grilled cheese and took one bite. He groaned loudly and started to push against the table with all his might. In a matter of seconds, his face contorted, and the color of his skin changed. He groaned even louder and then collapsed over the table. His eyes rolled back into his head, and now his skin had turned completely white. I held him in the chair, trying to feel for a heartbeat. I couldn't find a pulse. I frantically searched for any sign of life as panic washed over me. My daughter called for an ambulance, but I wondered if it was already too late. A great feeling of loss flooded over me as the gravity of the situation sunk in.

Right as I was starting to feel hopeless, I heard in my spirit, "The thief comes to steal, kill, and destroy, but I have come that you might have life and life abundantly."

I got so angry. I thought, *That dirty devil is trying to take him away from me.* I could feel righteous anger rise from my belly to my mouth as I shouted, "In the name of Jesus Christ of Nazareth, you spirit of death come out of Ervin!" Again, I shouted, pointing to the front door, "In the name of Jesus Christ of Nazareth, spirit of death, leave this house!" Then I shouted once more, "In the name of Jesus Christ of Nazareth, life come back!"

The moment the words left my mouth, Ervin took a deep breath for the first time since he had collapsed.

A few minutes later, the police came in. Ervin was still gray and unconscious, but he was breathing. They clamped on an oxygen mask while they waited for the paramedics to arrive.

They were trying to revive him while yelling, "Breathe deep! Breathe deep!"

There was no response. Finally, the ambulance came, and they placed him on a gurney to bring him to the hospital. While they were taking him out, he woke up.

Looking around, confused by all the commotion, he asked, "What are you doing to me?"

I tried to explain to him what was going on, but all the turmoil had him feeling disoriented and irritated.

———

When he arrived at the hospital, the doctors told us, "He's critical. We're taking him to intensive care because his blood pressure is sixty over zero."

I had no idea you could even be alive with blood pressure levels that low. As we headed over to the intensive care wing of the hospital, my two brothers, Jerry and Rome, walked in. Hope began to bubble up inside of me watching them walk down the hall. It felt as if two of God's warriors were coming to our aid. They had brought a Bible with them and I knew that in the hands of warriors, that weapon could slash down any sickness.

We all walked up to Ervin's room together, but the nurse said, "I'm sorry, but he's in such critical condition; only one of you can go in for a few minutes."

I said, "Okay, Rome, you go in."

The nurse said, "Well...I guess I could make an exception if two of you want to go."

So I said, "Alright, Jerry, you go with Rome."

The nurse happened to be a believer as well, and she

quickly realized we were all there to pray for him. She conceded and said, "Okay, you can all go in."

We all made our way into the room. Ervin was lying on the hospital bed with wires all over him. Rome laid his Bible on Ervin's chest and opened it to the Psalms. He prayed over Ervin, flipping to one verse after the other.

He would say in a confident proclamation, "Lord, Your Word says..." as he read each promise. "And Lord, Your Word also says..." he continued on declaring. He read Psalms 90:10 (NIV), which states, "Our days may come to seventy years, or eighty, if our strength endures..." Then he said, "Lord, Ervin hasn't even had seventy years yet, and You said in Your Word seventy or eighty if our strength endures." After that, he read Isaiah 53:5 and proclaimed, "By Your stripes, Lord, he is healed! He is healed!" When he finished praying, he told him, "Ervin, you're going to make it!"

Then my brother, Jerry, received a word from God, "The Lord says, 'I have healed you from the top of your graying head to the bottom of your feet.'"

Upon hearing this, I broke out in holy laughter. "Yes! Yes, Lord! He is healed." I laughed harder and harder to the point where it was uncontrollable. In that moment, I had such an assurance that God had already healed him.

The next day, they ran more tests to see how he was doing. The results shocked the hospital staff. His heart seemed to have a miraculous turnaround. The doctors wanted to monitor him for several more days after having such a major heart attack, but they told him if his health continued to be this good, then he could go home soon.

A few days later, we were packing up to leave the hospital. The doctor came in, still puzzled by the test results.

He stood there staring at the papers. "Do you think that we just thought it was worse than it actually was?"

I asked, "Well, what did the paramedics say when he came in? Wasn't his blood pressure critical?"

"Yeah, I know. I know, but this doesn't make sense!"

I reminded him that his blood pressure was only sixty over zero when he arrived.

The doctor remarked, "Yes, I see that, but how could he have been in such critical condition but now seem perfectly normal? I've done four sets of X-rays, and I ran four EKGs, but it doesn't even show any signs of a heart attack. It looks like nothing is even wrong with his heart."

I smiled on the inside, knowing it was Jesus who had healed him. "Well, Doctor, would you have to say then that it was prayer that made the difference?"

He didn't want to admit to the fact that Ervin's turn-around was a miracle, so he mumbled under his breath, "Well, since I have no other explanation, I guess so…"

AUTHOR'S NOTES:

If you've grown up in church, then I am sure you've heard it said that "the Lord gives and the Lord takes away." This theology is based on Job 1:21 (NIV), as Job himself says, "The Lord gave and the Lord has taken away…"

Up until this point, in Israelite culture, they believed that there was a singular operative power that brought life and death. Deuteronomy 32:39 (NIV) reinforces their belief, as God says to Israel, "…I put to death and I bring to life, I have wounded and I will heal…." God indeed did "smite" the Israelites, but this was never a fickle instance meant to "grow their character." It was always and solely in response to evil behavior. What I find incredible is that after the fall, mankind inherently deserved the consequences of sin, but God chose not to enforce them unless they *continued* in their evil behavior. Even in a hopeless state, God still paved the path for mankind to experience mercy and life.

> "This day I call the heavens and the earth as witnesses against you that I have set before you life and death, blessings and curses. Now choose life, so that you and your children may live and that you may love the Lord your God, listen to his voice, and hold fast to him. For the Lord is your life, and he will give you many years in the land he swore to give to your fathers, Abraham, Isaac and Jacob."

DEUTERONOMY 30:19–20 NIV

Despite our separated condition, He made life available to those who chose to enter into a relationship with Him—the very source of life itself. It stands to reason that if you reject the source of life, as the Israelites did, what else could be given? The only thing outside of God's good and perfect and life-giving nature is everything that He is not—which is why the Israelites experienced the bitter taste of death in their rebellion. If they rejected Him, then they were going to experience what life meant without Him: pain, illness, hopelessness, sin, and death.

Since the Israelites rejected God's ways of life so many times over the years, it became a pattern for their culture. They would sin, and God would respond in divine judgment. The Israelites would fall ill and experience famine and destruction by their enemies. Then they would come running back to God only to repeat the whole process all over again. Because of this cycle, they began to believe that sickness was the sole result of sin—hence why Job's friends frequently suggested this to him in their speeches. However, I believe the story of Job is placed in the Old Testament in order to derail their formulaic understanding of sickness.

The book opens by recounting Job as a blameless man who stayed away from evil and feared the Lord (see Job 1:1). The entire following narrative would have disrupted the Israelites' theology because they believed that negative circumstances were *solely* a result of sin. However, his story demonstrated that his onslaught was not a result of something he did.

From this whole ordeal, Job derives the theology in his questioning that "God gives and God takes away." However, the *narrator* of the story enlightens the reader that the following events were not due to the hand of a capricious God but rather something else that had its own agenda. The Scriptures recount, "So Satan went out from the presence of the Lord and afflicted Job..." (Job 2:7 NIV). It was satan who went out, *not* God. It seems as if this story was placed strategically in the Canonical Scriptures to reveal that there were other forces at work seeking to undermine God's *righteous* ones.

Although there were instances of God destroying something in the Bible, it was always something that was evil—never His righteous people. Furthermore, the Book of Job was written under an old covenant. Now, we are in a new covenant, and by the redemptive work of the cross, we have become the "righteousness of God" according to 2 Corinthians 5:21.

What God GIVES is LIFE, and what He TAKES (away) is our SIN (see John 3:16 and John 1:29).

We can confidently pray for the sick to be healed, demons to be cast out, and the dead to be raised because, as His body, we are commissioned to take part in destroying the works of the enemy. Jesus came to redeem us from our separated state and demolish the repercussions of our separation. His ministry made it clear that God's heart is to heal people. Sickness and disease are not part of His plan. If they were, then why did He go around annihilating them? (See Acts 10:38; Matthew 4:24; 9:35; Luke 6:19.) At some point, we go home to be with the Lord, but there is *no* Bible verse that says we have to go out sick!

In the end, satan failed, and God redeemed everything to Job, including his health. He even lived an additional 140 years after everything that happened. His days were full of abundance and life. My grandpa likewise lived a long, happy life after the devil tried to take him out before his time. My grandma boldly kicked out that foul spirit of death because she knew that it wasn't the Lord "taking" him home. He still had work here to do for Jesus. He went on to live another seventeen years after this story took place, and then, when it was his time, he returned to be home with the Lord.

CHAPTER 14
I JUST COULDN'T WAIT ANOTHER MINUTE!

For a few years, I became a representative for a company that sold beauty and personal care products. The company had assigned me a few blocks to cover. Every few weeks, I would stop in to check on my clients or to deliver their orders. When they saw me walking up the block, they would put on the coffee pot, and we would end up chatting for a while. The extrovert in me loved it! It was a great deal of fun getting to visit and meet all sorts of different people.

I remember one lady in particular, Marlys, who would always tell me her troubles every time I came by her house. She was on all sorts of medication: uppers, downers, and handfuls of pills for depression. Her marriage was just as bad. She and her husband would fight so viciously that their own family thought they would kill each other.

I really didn't know what to say when she would tell me about all the new problems she had each time I saw her. All these conversations took place before I had been filled with the Spirit, so I had no idea how to really help anyone. We need God's power to help set the captives free!

My best effort at the time was suggesting she should go to church. I would feel so sorry for her, but I didn't even have enough assurance of my own salvation at the time to really offer her any true hope. After every time we talked, I would sit in my car and cry for her. I was helpless, and so was she.

Everything changed once I was filled with the Holy Spirit. When you get filled, He gives you the power to witness to others.

> "But you will receive power when the Holy Spirit comes on you; and you will be my witnesses in Jerusalem, and in all Judea and Samaria, and to the ends of the earth."

> ACTS 1:8 NIV

Prior to this, I had never led anyone to the Lord in my life nor did I know how to share the gospel. After I was baptized in the Spirit, I still didn't know necessarily what I was doing, but I did know how to share my story of what the Lord had done for me. My testimony impacted people not just because of the words I shared but rather because they could see how the Lord changed the way I lived. I was a completely different person; I even carried myself differently. My life itself became the evidence of the gospel because people saw how it transformed everything about me. I was so filled up with joy that I couldn't stop laughing!

About two weeks after my baptism in the Spirit, Marlys called me to ask if we could go out for coffee. We met at a restaurant, and she shared her troubles like she usually did. However, this time, I wasn't weighed down by her problems. Instead, I was overcome with hope! In fact, I couldn't stop laughing because God had set me free. Joy was constantly bursting out of me.

I shared over coffee how God had healed me and delivered me from my prescription drug addiction. I quit taking tranquilizers because I had true peace now. I didn't feel helpless or hopeless anymore. I knew that if God could deliver me from my troubles, then He could also deliver Marlys from hers. I had a bold newfound confidence that God could turn any situation around. I had planned to pray for her that evening when we got in the car, but it completely slipped my mind.

The following week, she called and asked if we could go out again. The same thing happened; she shared how troubled she was, but I was still beaming with hope and joy. I drove her home again and parked in the driveway.

As we sat in the car, I said, "Marlys, are you a believer?" That was the only question I could think to ask.

She said, "Oh yes, yes. I'm a believer."

Since I didn't know how to address the root of her troubles, I simply prayed for peace.

As I backed out of the driveway after dropping her off, God spoke to me loud and clear, "You prayed wrong tonight. Marlys has to start at the beginning. But don't worry—My Holy Spirit will teach you."

I knew that Jesus meant she had to be born again. As Jack Winters put it, "I think many are conceived but not yet born." I believe that was the case with Marlys. Even though she had believed in Jesus, Jesus was not the Lord and Savior of her life...yet. I thought that she might be upset with me if I told her what I had heard the Lord say, but I decided I needed to do it either way.

A few days later, I invited her to church with me to

receive prayer from the pastor, who had prayed for me to be completely set free.

When I picked her up, I said, "Marlys, I've got to tell you something. The Lord showed me that you need to start at the beginning."

"Oh my goodness, that's what I've been thinking!"

Upon hearing her words, I let out a small sigh of relief. The Lord had already prepared the way. I knew that something great was going to happen that night.

Typically, after the service, people would line up to receive prayer from the pastor. Up front there was a single chair where someone would sit. The pastor had them sit first so they wouldn't fall. Many times, people couldn't stand under the weight of glory when they were receiving ministry. One by one, he prayed for each person.

Marlys was quite a shy lady. She kept holding onto me while we were waiting in line.

Over and over, she would say, "Now, you have to stay right here with me when I am getting prayed for. Don't leave my side."

All of a sudden, she let go of my hand and booked it as fast as she could for the front. She slid into that chair like a baseball player slides into home base. I was shocked, and I think so was everyone else in line. I started laughing because I could hardly believe that she would do anything like that, especially given her introverted personality.

When the pastor prayed for her, she was saved, healed, and filled with the Spirit all at once. The Lord healed her of migraines and stomach problems. She also got set free from all her drugs and delivered from all her mental health problems.

When the pastor finished praying for her, she walked

back to me and said, "I'm sorry. I just couldn't wait another minute! I knew I had to get prayed for right then!"

Marlys was a completely changed woman after that. Everyone could see it, especially her husband, Del. A few weeks later, Marlys received the gift of tongues while she was in her bedroom praying. Although she had been filled with the Spirit that night I took her to church, she wasn't able to speak in her heavenly language until now. After receiving the gift, she walked out of the bedroom, and Del saw her face glowing. Not only that, but every imperfection was turned into beauty. Del called us immediately. He kept repeating over the phone, "She's beautiful! Just beautiful! You have to come and see this." Even though he wasn't born again yet, I knew he was seeing her in the spirit.

He was so in awe of seeing her face glow with the presence of Jesus that he told his wife, "I don't know what in the world has happened to you, but whatever it is, I have to get it!"

My husband and I took Del and Marlys to the same church service. After the message, Del went forward, and the pastor prayed for him. He gave his life to Jesus, and God completely healed his body as well. He was supposed to have surgery because he had severe stomach issues, but when he went back to the doctor, they told him he no longer needed any surgery. From then on, his life was transformed.

———

Once a year, Marlys' mother, who lived several hours away, would make the trip to come visit them. When she came down to see her kids, the Lord impressed me to have the whole family come over for dinner. While I was making sure they felt welcomed and well taken care of in our home, my husband shared all about Jesus with them over the meal. Marlys' mom listened intently to each story because she knew something remarkable had happened to her daughter and son-in-law. Their marriage had turned around so dramatically that it served as the very evidence itself of the transformative power of the gospel. After knowing them for years, she could barely believe how different they seemed since her last visit.

The next day, Marlys' mom wanted me to stop over at the house for a visit to hear my story as well. While I was visiting with her, she opened up about all the health issues she had been facing. I could tell she was troubled by all of it. The anxiety surrounding her upcoming surgery weighed heavily on her. With hope in my eyes, I told her how God had supernaturally healed me. Tears streamed down her face as she listened to every word. I could tell the Lord was moving in her heart. I asked if she wanted to pray and give her life to Jesus.

She politely declined. "No, no. Not today."

I was confused. What was going on? She seemed ready to receive Jesus into her life. There was a genuine hunger in her eyes as she sat there listening to the gospel. I struggled to understand why she didn't want to be born again.

When I got back to my house, the phone rang. It was Marlys.

"Mother wants you to come at ten o'clock tomorrow. She'll be ready to accept the Lord then."

I chuckled on the inside; I thought it was funny that she wanted to make an appointment to receive Jesus. At ten o'clock sharp the next day, I arrived to find the house immaculate. Marlys' mom was dressed in her finest gown.

As I sat down with her, she remarked, "It wasn't proper yesterday. The house was a mess, and so was I. Now I'm ready."

That day, she received Jesus into her life as her Lord and Savior. She also got completely healed. When she went back to the doctors, they told her she no longer needed surgery. Do you know something…God loves healing people! God's heart is so big and merciful and compassionate; He longs to heal people. His desire to heal is so strong that it compelled Him to endure the brutal stripes on His back to freely give the priceless gift of healing (see Isaiah 53:5).

Del continued to walk faithfully with the Lord and was a man after God's heart. Marlys continued to shine brightly with the Holy Spirit all her days. They later told me that when God restored their marriage, it was as if they fell in love with one another all over again. The love they thought had once faded was rekindled to the sweetness and delight of what it had been in the beginning of their marriage. The power of the gospel transformed their whole family, even their children. Marlys was the first one who gave her life to Christ because of how Jesus transformed me. Many more salvations resulted because of our friendship over the years. The gospel spreads and multiplies like a wildfire; there is no stopping it!

AUTHOR'S NOTES:

"You yourselves are our letter, written on our hearts, known and read by everyone. You show that you are a letter from Christ, the result of our ministry, written not with ink but with the Spirit of the living God, not on tablets of stone but on tablets of human hearts."

2 CORINTHIANS 3:2–3 NIV

Our lives are like a letter constantly being read by those around us, but what does our letter say? Does it testify to the life-changing power of the gospel, or does it read exactly like a letter from the world? People are watching our lives and searching for hope. They are seeking to be freed from this curse of death that has been set in motion since the fall of Adam and Eve. People long for the redemptive touch of Jesus, who has the power to deliver us from drugs, heal our diseases, and restore our marriages. The good news is simple in application, practical in circumstance, and transformative in nature.

CHAPTER 15
REVIVAL IS ONE PHONE CALL AWAY

Growing up in the countryside in the 1940s meant sharing a water well with the neighbors. You would often find fathers standing around the well, talking and visiting with one another. When our father became a Christian, things began to change with the neighbors. When he walked over to the well, those standing around made fun of him and laughed.

One man in particular would always say mockingly, "Oh, here comes that holy man!"

Even though my father was constantly ridiculed for his faith by the neighbors, God was coordinating events beyond what our family could have imagined to reach the ones we never expected.

———

Fast-forward years later; I was filled with the Spirit and shortly after that, I made one phone call that ended up starting a series of events that I never saw coming.

I happened to be standing in my kitchen that day when

the Lord said to me out of the blue, "Call your aunt Onie and tell her what I have done for you."

I said, "Oh God, you have to be kidding!"

I was honestly in shock. I didn't know much about my aunt Onie, but from what I did know, I thought she would want nothing to do with Jesus. Up until that point, I had only shared my testimony with people who I thought would be interested in God. I never would have imagined that Aunt Onie would want to hear my story. Onie was quite a character who loved having a unique sense of fashion, but she was also a very fun and bubbly person to be around. Back in those days, she smoked, drank, and enjoyed all the pleasures of the party lifestyle.

The Lord said once again in a real gentle tone, "Just call her and tell her what I have done for you."

Being brand new at this, I insisted, "Lord, she's not interested." As if I knew better than God back in those days; I laugh thinking back on the whole story now.

God did not get mad with me for questioning Him; He simply persisted a third time.

I finally surrendered, but I said in a definite tone, "Okay, Lord, but I know she's not interested." I called my aunt and she answered the phone right away.

"Oh, hi Aunt Onie! I'm calling because…I have to tell you what's happened to me."

I began to share on the phone about receiving a miraculous healing from my accident and how God had delivered me from the fear I had suffered from my whole life. (See Chapter 2: "I Don't Know What In the World She's Got, but I Want It!")

As I shared, she would say excitedly, "Oh! Tell me more."

I began to tell her about my week with the Lord and all

the visions He showed me. I shared about everything I had experienced and how it changed me.

The more I shared with her, the more she would say, "Oh, that's so wonderful. Tell me some more."

Then I said something that even surprised me as the words came out of my mouth: "Well, I'll tell you what, I'm going to a lady's retreat this weekend. Would you like to come with me?"

She delightfully agreed.

————

Saturday morning rolls around, and here comes Aunt Onie walking up to the retreat center. Per her usual, she was dressed in something fashionable and daringly unique. I grew nervous as she walked up, wondering how some of the more "proper" and "ritzy" ladies at the retreat would receive her. To my relief, they all welcomed her with open arms and greeted her like she was part of the family. The whole day at the retreat was packed with listening to powerful speakers and fellowshipping with our sisters in Christ. After a full day, I was exhausted.

I had just crawled into bed when the Lord spoke to me, "This is your only chance to talk with your Aunt Onie."

I made my way back to her bunk in the cabin. She was lying in her bed, but she was still awake.

I asked, "Do you want to hear more of what Jesus showed me that week?"

Immediately, she jumped straight out of bed. "Yes!"

We made our way to the main hall so we could talk without disturbing the other ladies who wanted to sleep. Once we arrived in the large room, I started sharing more about what happened during that week and what God had been doing in my life since. After talking for about an hour, I asked her if she wanted to have a relationship with Jesus. With hunger and excitement in her eyes, she nodded.

At this point, it was around midnight when we started to pray. We happened to be sitting with our backs faced away from the window. It was pitch black behind us. When I prayed with Onie to receive Jesus and be set free, I heard the most eerie scratching against the window screen. I did not dare turn around and look, but I immediately knew it was demonic spirits. Their intense clawing sent shivers down my spine, but I kept praying until finally, it ceased.

The next morning, she woke up before me and headed to the bathroom to get ready alongside all the other ladies. When I made my way there, I found them all standing around rejoicing because she had told them that she had accepted Christ.

One of the ladies joyfully remarked, "I was praying for you when you both got up to leave because I knew that was the moment you were going to have the opportunity to receive Jesus."

———

After the retreat, I brought Onie back home to downtown Minneapolis. When we stepped in the door, I could see that it was an absolute mess. No matter where you looked, trash was everywhere, and mounds of things were piled up. Ashtrays and empty bottles filled her table. There was not even one clear spot on it.

She turned to me and said, "I don't know one thing

about the Bible. Let's have a Bible study here so I can learn. You have to teach me!"

I had never led a Bible study before since I was pretty new to all this myself, but I agreed, and we set a date that week to host one in her house. I was excited about what God was doing in her, but I was not looking forward to attempting to navigate through downtown Minneapolis again. Back then, there were no such things as GPS or cell phones, so finding my way through the big city was very intimidating.

That Wednesday, I was on my way to her place again, but being alone this time, I got lost. I was so flustered trying to figure out where I was that I thought it would be a miracle just to find her house.

I told the Lord on my drive, "I'll only go this time, but I'm never coming back here!"

Well, what a joke that turned out to be because we ended up having Bible studies regularly in that very house for years.

I still remember the shock I felt when I walked in that door again a few days later—the house was absolutely immaculate. It almost looked like a different home alto-gether. When I looked at Aunt Onie, she looked as brand new as the house. Everything had entirely changed since I last saw her.

Onie had invited her daughter Leota to come, as well as another distant relative of mine, Vonnie. It was only the four of us at our very first Bible study. I started sharing about the power of the name of Jesus. As I preached, suddenly, Leota started groaning in pain. Within minutes, her pain turned to agony and from agony into absolute misery. Little did I know that she had been struggling with kidney stones.

As Onie was helping her to a nearby bedroom to lie down, she said, "We might have to call for the doctor. When she gets this bad, they give her morphine until the pain passes."

Another few minutes had gone by when we heard Leota wailing from the severe symptoms. All of us rushed over to her bedroom. She was hunched over on the bed from the pain.

Onie turned to me in desperation and said, "Oh, please pray for her."

I had never prayed for healing for anybody in my life. I knew it was possible because the Lord had healed me, but I didn't know how to pray for healing for others yet. I knelt down on the hardwood floors and laid my hand on Leota. I said the shortest prayer of healing because I didn't know what to say, but I knew to pray in the name of Jesus because there is power in His name!

In one minute, Leota went from screaming to sobbing to sound asleep. We all stood there staring in shock over such a sudden change after praying. After a moment, we slipped out of the room and headed back to the kitchen to resume our Bible study.

Vonnie started crying and said, "I need Jesus!"

After witnessing what happened to Leota, faith was birthed in her heart. She saw that Jesus was the Healer. After we led her to the Lord, she wanted us to pray for her bowed leg. As we prayed, her crooked knee completely straightened out.

At the time, Vonnie had been working as a waitress in a restaurant. All her coworkers constantly witnessed her bowleg as she moved about the restaurant, especially when she went up and down the stairs. After she was healed, all her coworkers were shocked to see that now her crooked leg was as straight as the other. She began to share her testimony with them, and God began to move in her workplace.

Her physical healing became a big part of her testimony, as well as her freedom from a lifetime of emotional pain. At this time, she was in her forties, but her childhood was very traumatic, to say the least. She and her sister, Elva, suffered from horrible abuse. Sadly, it caused a lot of dysfunction in her own family. Her kids became troubled growing up in a turbulent household.

After she gave her life to Jesus, everything completely changed. She shared the gospel with her kids, and a few of them became born again and turned their lives around as well. Shortly after that, her first husband passed away, and she remarried to a wonderful Christian man. They ended up starting a powerful prison ministry to share the good news with prisoners all over the country.

Vonnie came to Christ simply by witnessing a miracle happen to someone else. It planted a seed of faith in her own life to see firsthand the Lord's miracle-working power. This is why the gifts of the Holy Spirit are crucial for today. It is for the salvation of souls! Not only did she give her life to Christ but she ended up leading many more people to Jesus because she had also experienced the power of God.

———

After a while, Leota woke up and entered the kitchen where we were sitting.

She cried out, "I want Jesus!"

Leota gave her life to Jesus that night as well. It was an amazing first Bible study. After that meeting, many people came to hear about the good news. Throughout the months that followed, Onie invited all of her friends to come and experience Jesus. All kinds of fish came—from partiers to gang members to people who desperately needed the redemptive power of God.

At one of our weekly meetings, we were praying for the salvation of the souls of those we personally knew who had not yet received the Lord.

One of the ladies spoke up and asked, "Can we pray for my boyfriend, Louie?"

Another one had chimed in, "Oh, yeah, I know Louie's sister."

"Well, let's pray for the salvation of the whole family," I said. "How many are there?"

There happened to be a total of sixteen kids in the Coleman family since both parents had remarried and entered into their new marriage with eight kids each. That night, we claimed all sixteen of them for the Lord in prayer. It wasn't long before Louie came to the Bible study to check it out for himself.

As the night progressed, I turned to Louie and said, "Do you want to see God do something?"

Not knowing what to expect, he politely agreed. This Bible study was Louie's first exposure to Jesus. His family had never heard of the gospel before or even knew that miracles were possible.

In that moment, I sensed that God wanted to show Louie His miracle-working power. I called my aunt over to where Louie and I were sitting. She had suffered from a bad limp most of her life and I felt that, tonight, God was going to heal it.

I said, "Onie, let's check to see if your legs are uneven."

Sure enough, one of her legs was two inches shorter

than the other. As we prayed, her leg shot out in front of our eyes. Louie was so terrified at the sight that he ran out of the house. I had never seen someone run so fast; it was hilarious! We all sat there laughing.

Later that night, he called my house to talk about what happened. My husband picked up the phone because I was just getting home from the meeting. I motioned to him to share the gospel with Louie while he was on the phone. He told him about the wonderful news of Jesus and right then and there, Louie gave his life to Christ. He was the first one of the sixteen to get saved.

———

A few months later, Onie called me one evening crying, "I got home from work, and I got a call that Ramona Coleman is in the hospital. Her husband walked out on her, and she took a whole bottle of pills. Her kids found her unconscious on the bathroom floor. They ran from house to house seeking help until, finally, someone listened and came to see what had happened. The neighbors brought her straight to the hospital." (This took place long before we had things like 9-1-1.)

She continued, "I got there, and the doctors said, 'She won't wake up. She has not responded at all since she arrived.' I went into the hospital room, not knowing what to expect, but here she was, lying wide awake in bed. Since she had a trachea in her throat, she could not speak, but she seemed very conscious. I shared my testimony with her about how I found Jesus, and then I told her about the gospel. I asked her if she had ever made peace with God, and she shook her head. So then I asked her if she would like to, and she nodded. Even though she could not speak as I prayed with her, I could see in her body language that she was receiving every bit of what I was praying. Laughter began to bubble up from within her as the Lord filled her with His joy. You could see something shift in her eyes. Her face started to glow with the most beautiful light, and then she went back to sleep. I don't know if I did everything right…this is my first time leading someone to Jesus. What if I missed something? Will you come and pray for her?"

When my aunt told me the story, I knew she had led Ramona to the Lord, but she was worried because she was new at all of this, and she wanted me to make sure. I decided to go to the hospital to reassure her. When I arrived, Ramona's family members were in the waiting room. Around twenty of them stood around waiting for her to wake up. Onie and I headed to Ramona's room to see if she was awake, but we found her absolutely sound asleep.

She never woke up when we were there, but I sensed as I prayed that she had already found the Lord. A few days later, she went home to be with Jesus. The only time she was conscious in the hospital was when the Lord had impressed Onie to go see her. We had prayed a few months prior for the entire family's salvation, and now Jesus had paved the way for Ramona to hear the gospel before she could have been lost forever.

After we left the room, we talked with her family for a little while and prayed for several of them before driving home. As a result of that, a few days later, someone from the family called me to ask if I would come to the wake.

Onie, my husband, and I all made our way downtown to the sizeable four-level house where the service was being held. When we walked in, we saw that the place was absolutely packed with people. Some were sitting on stairs, others playing cards at different tables, and some were merely standing around. Even though there were people everywhere you looked, the atmosphere itself was as hushed as a library. It gave you the kind of feeling where you did not want to speak, fearing the fact that everyone in the room could hear your voice blaring against the stillness. As we stood quietly in the house, someone approached me to ask if I knew how to say prayers. I nodded, and they asked if I could share something for the service right now.

When I raised my voice to speak, the room went from a hushed muffled sound to an absolute dead silence. You could hear a pin drop. Everyone was all ears now. I started by sharing the story about Onie leading Ramona to the Lord. I explained with Scripture why I knew Ramona was in heaven with Jesus. I talked about the power of the gospel and then prayed for the entire group.

Afterward, I went around and talked with different people individually. I handed out a few things like Bibles and gospel tracts to anyone who wanted to hear more. One of the individuals told us that Ramona's dad had recently had a heart attack, and he was upstairs in bed still ill from the incident. My husband headed up the stairs to see if he could pray for him.

He found him in one of the bedrooms, looking depleted of life. His partying lifestyle had caught up to him. My husband was moved with compassion and started sharing his testimony with him. He talked about how God had delivered him from partying and heavy drinking and how God desires to save us from the things that are actually trying to kill us. After sharing with him for a while, he prayed for him, and then we left the wake.

A few weeks later, the Lord spoke to me, "Go see the Coleman family." The parents and some of the kids lived on the Indian reservation west of the cities. It was a two-day round trip to go see them. Being a mother of three, I didn't know how I could make the time to go. I asked God when I should go, and He instantly replied, "Friday." It happened to be the perfect timing because my husband was able to watch the kids while I was gone. Isn't it amazing how the Lord can coordinate even the most practical of details?

When I told my aunt Onie that I was going to visit the Coleman family, she insisted on coming with me. That Friday, we headed up to the reservation. We decided to bring gospel tapes, worship music, and all sorts of gifts for their family. When we arrived, we sat in the living room and visited with the parents as they opened the different presents we had brought.

Within a few minutes, Mr. Coleman, who we had prayed with a few weeks earlier at the wake, said, "I'm so afraid to die."

I gave a light-hearted laugh and looked at him, "Well, you don't have to be."

I shared the good news with him and explained why we can look forward to meeting Jesus face-to-face in heaven one day. I told him about the glorious paradise that awaits those who put their faith in Him. With hunger in his eyes, he told me that he wanted this kind of hope that only Jesus offered.

His wife began crying, "Oh, I need that too!"

So, we prayed for both of them right then and there to receive Jesus. When we finished, they asked if we would go in and talk with their daughter, Dixie. She had been very depressed since her sister, Ramona, had died.

I walked over to her room and immediately upon entering, I noticed how dark it was. It was a darkness that wasn't merely physical; rather, it was a spiritual heaviness that overtook the place. Something gloomy and evil filled that room.

I could see the outline of a person underneath a pile of blankets. I sat on the edge of the bed and started to tell Dixie how much God loved her. As I kept talking, she began to pull the blankets down just enough so I could see her eyes peering back at me. Dixie didn't say a word, but she kept looking intently at me as she listened.

I told her about the wonderful news of Jesus, and I asked if she would like to be born again. She agreed, and I prayed with her. As soon as I finished praying, she sat right up. I saw that her arms were all bandaged up from attempting suicide by cutting herself. Moved with compassion, I asked her if she had ever seen God do anything. She shook her head no.

God had given me a gift of faith for seeing legs grow out, so I said, "Let's check your legs."

Sure enough, one was shorter than the other. I prayed and commanded the leg to grow. She was absolutely blown away by seeing her leg grow just like her brother Louie had been a few months prior.

A few minutes after I had left the room, Dixie came out all dressed up, looking like an entirely different person.

Her parents stared in shock. "What did you do to her?"

I simply smiled, knowing it was Jesus who had completely transformed her. It wasn't anything I could have done.

My other aunt, Polly, happened to live near the Coleman family, so I thought while we were up in the area, we'd go see her too. On our way to her house, we stopped in at a restaurant to grab a bite to eat. While we were there, I saw a woman sitting in the bar section of the diner.

I heard the Lord whisper, "Go and tell that woman I love her."

At that very moment, some of Onie's old friends happened to be at the restaurant. They came over to say hi. I hesitated, not wanting to be rude while they were talking to us, but out of the corner of my eye, I saw the woman get up and leave. I thought surely I missed my opportunity to go talk with her.

Once we finished visiting with Onie's friends, we walked outside to leave. Sitting on the bench beside the restaurant was the woman I felt led to talk to. I walked up to her and said exactly what God had told me. I happened to have a little Billy Graham tract on me, and I gave it to her. I shared a little bit, but I felt like God only wanted me to plant a seed in that moment.

Onie had grown up in that area, so she knew almost everyone. When we got back to the car, she told me, "That's the town prostitute."

God wants everyone to know how much He loves them! You never know who may need to hear it. Keep listening to the Father's voice, and He will show you.

When we arrived at my aunt Polly's house, her husband opened the door. He was not a big fan of guests nor a big fan of his wife. He was a grumpy old man.

In a grumbling tone, he remarked, "She's already in bed. She's in pain."

We went into the bedroom anyway to see if we could visit with her for a little while. When we walked in, we saw her little old body lying there as she moaned in pain.

I don't know why I did this, but I told her, "Why don't you sit up on this chair here and we'll pray for you."

The chair was a short distance away on the other side of the bedroom, but my aunt was in so much pain that it took her five minutes to hobble over from the bed to the chair. She looked terribly sad. You could tell her entire body ached. If misery was a person, it was my aunt Polly at that very moment. After she sat down in the chair, we knelt beside her to pray. Onie and I spoke in agreement that she would be completely healed in Jesus' name. She started yelling and waving her arms in the air. Then she shot up out of the chair and started kicking her legs all over. Onie and I were so shocked that we went into hysterical holy laughter.

As she twirled about, dancing all over that room, she shouted loud enough for the neighbors to hear, "Pain free! Pain free! Pain free!"

It seemed surreal to watch her prance around since, moments before, she could barely walk. We were so weak in the knees from laughing that we tumbled onto the floor. Our stomachs were cramping from the intensity of joy!

I can witness to the fact that anything is possible with God! Just because you're old doesn't mean you have to be in pain. God can set you free and get you dancing!

———

A few months after our road trip, my friend Marlys (from the previous chapter) wanted to go see her sister-in-law, Dottie, who was in a mental health care center. I had talked to Onie on the phone in the meantime, and she suggested I see one of her friends, Joan, as well when I went to visit Dottie since they were staying in the same hospital. Joan had been admitted a few months prior because she had a mental breakdown on a bus, and now, she had been in rehab ever since.

When Marlys and I arrived, they told us that Dottie was with a counselor right now, so we would have to wait.

I said, "Let's go see Joan then in the meantime."

We walked upstairs and everywhere you looked there was the color gray. Cold gray cement floors and gray-painted walls covered everything in sight. It was depressing. Every once in a while, you would see someone shuffling through the hall with their head down. It was heartbreaking to see each patient look lost in their own world of drugs.

When we arrived at Joan's area, I peered through the door's small window that allowed you to see inside the room. I could see her sitting on the bed, looking as sad as everyone else on that floor. The nurse told us how critical she was and assured us that it would be months before she ever got out of here.

As we walked inside, we could hear the door lock behind us. It felt like a prison. I couldn't imagine what life would be like to be stuck in this dull room day after day. The atmosphere was so dreary. My eyes traced the room, and I realized that the only possession she had in here was a small twin bed. Even I started to feel sad as I looked around.

On the drive up to the hospital, I bought a little present for her. I had stopped in a small shop and saw a nice pair of house slippers. I didn't know what size she was, but the

Lord knew. I handed her the present, and she tried on the slippers.

Overjoyed at seeing them, she remarked, "They fit perfectly! They are exactly what I needed!"

I started to tell her about the good news of Jesus Christ, and shortly into our conversation, she gladly accepted the Lord. I prayed for her deliverance, and instantly, her mind became sound. A mere two days later, they ended up releasing her because she was perfectly healthy.

She told me later on that when we had walked into her room at the ward that day, she saw the light come in. Everywhere we go, we carry that light. Jesus said in Matthew 5:14 that we are the light of the world. There are many people who need a touch from the light of Jesus.

After we finished visiting with Joan, we were able to go see Dottie.

As we sat and talked with her, tears streamed down her face. "They told me I'm incorrigible. I'll never get free. I'm an impossible case."

Thankfully, words like *incorrigible* and *impossible* do not exist in the dictionary of God's Kingdom. Dottie also got saved, set free, and delivered that day by the power of Jesus. Praise God!

———

It's hard to imagine that so much happened from just *one* phone call to my aunt Onie. I'm sure only in heaven will I get to witness the full ripple effect of that one small act of obedience. Now, you may be wondering, what does all of this have to do with the story I shared at the beginning about my dad being mocked by the neighbors? Well, there's one salvation that happened at that Bible study in my aunt's house that I haven't shared yet.

There was a young girl in her twenties named Marilyn who came to our Bible studies. She was in a gang at the time and had heard about our meetings through her sister Joan. She had recently been released from prison after helping rob a bank. When she heard about the good news, she surrendered her life to Jesus and moved to a small town to try to escape her gang in Minneapolis.

If you know anything about Minnesota, then you know that we have horribly long and harsh winters with months of snow. When plows come through and clear the roads and parking lots, they create giant snowbanks all over. Shortly after she had given her life to the Lord, Marilyn and her boyfriend had unknowingly backed up against a snowbank and the exhaust began to leak into their car. They ended up dying that day from asphyxiation.

When I heard the news, I was so upset, but the Lord spoke to me, "I said whosoever will, may come, and Marilyn came. She never turned from Me. Man looks on the outward, but I see the heart. Marilyn has entered into glorious light. She has been set free."

Several years later, a good friend of mine who had moved outside of the city happened to be in Minneapolis working on a job. She called me and asked if we could go out for dinner together to catch up. While we were out to eat, the first thing she brought up was this man she was working with. She went on to share how troubled he was and how he would always confide in her. The main source of his discontentment was the death of his young sister. She had passed away several years earlier, and he always wondered where his sister was after she had died.

Finally, I asked, "Well, what's his sister's name?"

"Marilyn," she replied.

With all the details she had already shared, I began to connect the dots. This wasn't just any Marilyn; this was *the* Marilyn that I had led to Jesus a few months before she had gone on to be with the Lord.

"Oh my goodness! I know her."

In fact, not only did I know her, I also knew her parents. I realized that this man and his two sisters, Joan and Marilyn, were the children of the very man who used to make fun of my father at the well and mock, "Here comes that holy man!"

After we finished talking, I ended up calling their brother to share with him how his sister, Marilyn, had given her life to the Lord before she passed away. He was so relieved to hear that she was in heaven with Jesus.

Isn't it amazing how God has a way of working all things together for good in the end? Even though Marilyn's dad once ridiculed our family for being Christians, we ended up leading both of his daughters to the Lord.

God is constantly weaving together situations to draw people back into a relationship with Him. God truly desires that *none* should perish! His plan has always been to redeem people, and *you* are part of that great plan! So, go! Go and preach, saying the Kingdom of Heaven is here. Heal the sick, raise the dead, cleanse the lepers, and drive out demons because freely you have received, and now it is the time to freely give.

AUTHOR'S NOTES:

People may mock Godly families for their faith, but out of Godly families come Godly children who go on to share the light of Christ with people. As people see the light, they are drawn to Christ and become born again. In their transformation, it begins to transform not only themselves but also their families and communities, as well as their schools and their workplaces. They go on to reach the prisons and the mental wards, as well as the suicidal and the depressed. They reach those in desperate need of a Savior, as well as those who may not even have been looking for one. The gospel has been spreading and will continue to spread until it reaches everyone. There is no stopping it. As you've read from this book, evangelism, miracles, healings, and the supernatural are for *every* believer. It is not only for those who stand on a stage or go to a different country. It is for the bus drivers, the corporate salesmen, the moms, the blue-collar workers, the high school teachers—it is for everyone.

He came to pour out His Spirit UPON THEM ALL.

> "'In the last days,' God says, 'I will pour out my Spirit upon all people. Your sons and daughters will prophesy. Your young men will see visions, and your old men will dream dreams. In those days I will pour out my Spirit even on my servants—men and women alike—and they will prophesy.'"

ACTS 2:17–18 NLT

These are the days. His Spirit has been poured out so that we may be His witnesses to every part of the earth (see Acts 1:8). The power of the gospel is for the young and old, for men and women. It is for every believer. If you are a believer, then the same Christ who healed all who came to Him, destroyed the works of the devil, and brought the

Kingdom for everyone to experience His redemptive touch is now living in you!

> "I have been crucified with Christ and I no longer live, but Christ lives in me. The life I now live in the body, I live by faith in the Son of God, who loved me and gave himself for me."

GALATIANS 2:20 NIV

He is the same God today as He was when He walked on this earth. Now, He continues His work through *you*, His body. Our lives are no longer our own. There are still the remains of the enemy's destruction on this earth, but the strong man has been bound. Now we are called to gather the spoils of victory (see Luke 11:21–23). Now is the time to plunder hell and populate heaven. It is our duty as soldiers of Christ to help those who are perishing.

> "Go and rescue the perishing! Be their savior! Why would you stand back and watch them stagger to their death? And why would you say, "But it's none of my business"? The one who knows you completely and judges your every motive is also the keeper of souls—and not just yours! He sees through your excuses and holds you responsible for failing to help those whose lives are threatened."

PROVERBS 24:11–12 TPT

One does not go to war to save their own life, one goes to save the lives of others. You can ignore the darkness around you, but I assure you, it will *not* be ignoring you. We are in a war, whether we want to see it or not. Now is not the time to stay within the comforts of our church walls. We must leave behind the fear of what people may think of us. We must abandon the mentality that says someone else will reach that person in our lives who we know needs Jesus.

You are the roster of heaven. You are the soldier called to active duty. You are God's body on the earth. There is still a massive labor shortage, but a generation could rise to the occasion and end the shortage. Together, we could choose to be a people that ensures the love of God reaches every corner of the earth—including our own corner.

The question remains: will you be wise? You may be wondering, what does wisdom have to do with it? My friend, you must brush up on your Proverbs:

> "But a life lived loving God bears lasting fruit, for the one who is truly wise wins souls."

> PROVERBS 11:30 TPT

As believers, we have all been given this glorious Kingdom to share with everyone, but will you *bury* it, or will you *build* it?

THE BEST NEWS OF ALL, FOR ALL

HOW TO BECOME BORN AGAIN

I wanted to include this section specifically for those readers who may not be familiar with the gospel, or perhaps you have heard about Jesus, but you have never encountered Him in the way He is presented in these pages. Maybe this is the first time you've learned that God is the One who can heal you. Or that He is the One who can fill you up with so much joy that you can't help but laugh. Or that He is the One who can give you the wisdom you need for everyday life situations. Or that He is the One who can set you free. Or that He is the One who simply desires to be your friend.

I find there are a lot of people who have an idea of what God may be like, but there are still so many who do not know the simple and profound truth that He is a personal God who longs to have a *relationship* with us. The heart of the gospel is about restoring mankind's relationship with our Heavenly Father, who created us all. Jesus came because we were separated from God after Adam and Eve sinned. When Jesus gave His life for us, He made a way for each person to be restored to the Father. All along, God's heart has been to redeem His people as He intended them to be.

In fact, that's what the very word *righteousness* reflects. If you've grown up in church, then you may have heard it preached that righteousness means "to be in right standing with God." This is true and an important aspect of righteousness, but if we also say that God is righteous…then who is He in right standing with? This word in the original language encompasses a richly layered meaning—at its heart, it means "to be as you ought to be." That of course raises the question: *how are we supposed to be?* Well…God designed us to reflect Him! He made us in His image and with His qualities, but we lost this identity in the fall of man.

In the garden, Adam and Eve disobeyed God and listened to the serpent (aka the devil) instead (see Genesis 3). When they chose to follow the serpent's suggestion of eating the fruit from the tree of the knowledge of good and evil, they made a pivotal decision that would affect the entire world. This costly act of turning away from God's design set death in motion. Their bond with the Creator was painfully severed, and now the whole world would taste the bitter fruit of what life was like disconnected from God's life-giving Presence.

> "When Adam sinned, the entire world was affected. Sin entered human experience, and death was the result. And so death followed this sin, casting its shadow over all humanity, because all have sinned."

ROMANS 5:12 TPT

The world became separated from the very source of

life, hope, joy, peace, truth, and love itself. Mankind became quite awful, and even to this day, we still see the horrible effects of this sin. You don't have to look far to notice the brokenness, pain, sickness, and evil of this world. We are honestly hopeless without God.

All the time, people try to earn their way back to "goodness," but the reality is we just don't have it in our own nature to do it. Even in our effort to try to "live a good enough life" in hopes of ending up in a "good place" one day, we then imply that God *owes us* "salvation" because of *our* effort. But God would never place Himself in the debt of any man or woman. Salvation cannot be earned and there is no possible way for us to pay for the debt *we owe* God. The consequence of this debt is death because that is the payment for sin—the wages of death.

> "For sin's meager wages is death, but God's lavish gift is life eternal, found in your union with our Lord Jesus, the Anointed One."

> ROMANS 6:23 TPT

Sin requires a sacrifice because there are consequences for evil and harmful actions. If there weren't, then there would be no sense of justice in the world. God is a perfectly just judge, but He is also a loving and merciful God. So, God Himself provided a means of reconciliation by giving His perfect Son to pay for mankind's debt. Jesus was the *only one* who could bear the entire sin of the world, even the future sins that were to be committed. He made the final payment for everyone's "debt" once and for all on the cross by becoming the ultimate sacrifice. He took on the consequences by dying in our place.

"But Christ proved God's passionate love for us by dying in our place while we were still lost and ungodly! And there is still much more to say of his unfailing love for us! For through the blood of Jesus we have heard the powerful declaration, 'You are now righteous in my sight.' And because of the sacrifice of Jesus, you will never experience the wrath of God. So if while we were still enemies, God fully reconciled us to himself through the death of his Son, then something greater than friendship is ours. Now that we are at peace with God, and because we share in his *resurrection* life, how much more we will be rescued from sin's dominion! And even more than that, we overflow with triumphant joy in our new relationship of living reconciled to God—all because of Jesus Christ!"

ROMANS 5:8–11 TPT

Out of His great love, He offered us the <u>free gift</u> of forgiveness, salvation, righteousness, and eternal life. He paid for what we never could have. It is His gift to us. It is not something that can ever be earned; it is only received *by faith.* If we choose to place our faith in Him and believe that His sacrifice is enough to make us right with God, then His blood will wash away our sins, never to be remembered again.

"For I will demonstrate my mercy to them and will forgive their evil deeds, and never remember again their sins."

HEBREWS 8:12 TPT

We can be completely forgiven because *Jesus* already took on the consequences for it all. He took on what you deserved so that you could have what He deserved, but why did He do this? Why did the Father allow His Son to be sacrificed? Why did the Son allow Himself to go through such a brutally painful death on the cross? It was because of *love*. God LOVES you! It wasn't "reason" that moved the heart of God; the cross was the most unreasonable, unfair event in the history of the world. Yet, Jesus came to earth to represent the image of the invisible God— the Father—to show the world that the Father's heart longs to have a relationship with us.

> "The Son is the image of the invisible God, the firstborn over all creation."

> COLOSSIANS 1:15 NIV

> "Jesus answered, 'I am the way and the truth and the life. No one comes to the Father except through me. If you really know me, you will know my Father as well. From now on, you do know him and have seen him.'"

> JOHN 14:6–7 NIV

> "All this is from God, who reconciled us to himself through Christ and gave us the ministry of reconciliation: that God was reconciling the world to himself in Christ, not counting people's sins against them. And he has committed to us the message of reconciliation."

> 2 CORINTHIANS 5:18–19 NIV

Jesus revealed the Father's heart through the ultimate display of love—which is sacrifice.

> "There is no greater love than to lay down one's life for one's friends."

JOHN 15:13 NLT

Jesus went through the most excruciating death on the cross so that you did not have to taste the sting of death that was set into motion after the fall. He made the final triumph over sin and death when He rose from the dead three days later! He is alive! He triumphed over sin, sickness, hell, and the grave! When we surrender our lives to Christ, this "old nature" from Adam dies! Essentially, we get a do-over. We receive a brand new nature. This is why Jesus came, so we could be righteous, aka "how He intended us to be." Now, we can also be raised to life because of Christ's victory and experience this triumph over sin and death.

> "Sharing in his death by our baptism means that we were co-buried with him, so that when the Father's glory raised Christ from the dead, we were also raised with him. We have been co-resurrected with him so that we could be empowered to walk in the freshness of new life. For since we are permanently grafted into him to experience a death like his, then we are permanently grafted into him to experience a resurrection like his and the new life that it imparts. Could it be any clearer that our former identity is now and forever deprived of its power? For we were co-crucified with him to dismantle the stronghold of sin within us, so that we would not continue to live one

moment longer submitted to sin's power. Obviously, a dead person is incapable of sinning. And if we were co-crucified with the Anointed One, we know that we will also share in the fullness of his life."

ROMANS 6:4–8 TPT

When we repent, it means we are no longer under the devil's dominion, which only produces death, because we are choosing to live in God's ways which lead to life instead. This is simply what repentance means—"to turn." Adam and Eve turned away from God's design, but because of Jesus, we have the opportunity to turn back and be restored to the Father. He will teach you all about His ways of living—trust me, they are much better than ours! His Kingdom is joy, peace, and righteousness (see Romans 14:17). Essentially, it is everything He is and everything He intended for us.

When we are in a relationship with Him, we never die because we are connected to the very source of eternal life. One day, we will enter into the glorious paradise that He is preparing for us in heaven, but while we are on earth, we can also experience the power of His redemption because we can now live in His Kingdom that He brought to earth, essentially it is the *King's Domain*.

"For he has rescued us from the dominion of darkness and brought us into the kingdom of the Son he loves, in whom we have redemption, the forgiveness of sins."

COLOSSIANS 1:13–14 NIV

If we invite Him, His Spirit will come live inside of us

and give us this glorious inheritance of a new nature—His nature.

> "Everything we could ever need for life and godliness has already been deposited in us by his divine power. *For all this was lavished upon us* through the rich experience of knowing him who has called us by name and invited us to come to him through a glorious manifestation of his goodness. As a result of this, he has given you magnificent promises that are beyond all price, so that through *the power of* these tremendous promises we can experience partnership with the divine nature, by which you have escaped the corrupt desires that are of the world."

> 2 PETER 1:3–4 TPT

His Holy Spirit will empower you to live as a righteous person set free from the power of sin and your old ways of living. That old man or woman who desired to sin <u>dies</u> and you become born again as an entirely new creation. This is why it is important to be baptized with water after you give your life to Jesus because it symbolizes the reality of this. It is a symbol of your "old nature" dying underneath the water and the new creation that you are as you arise.

> "This means that anyone who belongs to Christ has become a new person. The old life is gone; a new life has begun!"

> 2 CORINTHIANS 5:17 NLT

When you are born into God's family, He writes your

name in His special book of life. If you decide to turn your life toward Him and fully surrender to Him as Lord, you will experience the hope, joy, peace, and love you've always longed for. If you would like to surrender your life right now to God and enter into a relationship with Him, then you can pray this out loud:

"Dear Lord Jesus Christ, I call upon Your name! Thank You for giving Your life as a sacrifice for me. I believe that You are the Son of God and that You died and rose again so that I might be forgiven and experience eternal life. Please forgive me. Wash away all my sins with Your precious blood and break every chain. I repent from my old ways of living. Teach me Your ways Heavenly Father. I put my faith in You alone. I believe in my heart what I speak with my mouth: Jesus is now my Lord and Savior, and I belong to Him. Jesus, I invite You now to come live inside of me. Fill me with the power of Your Holy Spirit. In Jesus' name I ask, Amen!"

Thank you for reading *Upon Them All*!

We'd love to hear how this collection of testimonies has impacted you. Please visit our website at: https://www.ellianaolivia.com/connect

If you are interested in exploring more of my work, including future projects and writings, please visit: https://www.ellianaolivia.com/shop

If these stories of God's miraculous work have ignited your faith and encouraged your walk with Jesus, please consider sharing your reflections on Amazon, Goodreads, or another platform. Your review helps others discover the hope and transformative power of God.